Breaking Out of The Change Trap

A Practical Guide for Organizational Change

Ron Rosenberg

Roberta J. Buland, Editor
Christianne L. Smith, Cover Design

BANBURY PRESS
Raleigh, North Carolina

First Edition

BANBURY PRESS
Raleigh, NC 27624

Editor: Roberta J. Buland
Cover Design: Christianne L. Smith
Graphic Design: Lorie B. Rosenberg

ISBN: 1-887980-01-6

Library of Congress Catalog Number: 98-93253

BANBURY PRESS books are available at quantity discounts for premiums, sales promotions, or in corporate training programs. Write to the Director of Marketing, P.O. Box 99451, Raleigh, NC 27624-9451, or in the
U.S. or Canada call 800-260-0662. From other locations call 919-847-
0662. You may fax requests to 919-847-9041.

Acknowledgments

Breaking Out of the Change Trap is the result of a great many experiences with a wide variety of organizations and an even wider variety of people. While it is impossible to thank everyone who helped shape this book, several individuals deserve individual recognition.

Gary Bishop, Bob Deeter, Linda Furgerson, Ramses Girgis, and Mark Van Zandt all reviewed preliminary copies of the manuscript and provided valuable feedback and suggestions that helped improve the overall quality of the book.

Roberta Buland, my editor, made many changes in both grammar and content that improved the readability and flow of the book and helped clearly present our message to the reader.

Roger Bushnell and Cary Ludwig, two of my managers during my employment at Nortel, demonstrated through their actions that large organizations can effect meaningful change and produce tangible business results.

Cher Holton, who also reviewed the book, has been a colleague and friend since we founded QualityTalk®. Her insights and ideas have helped our business develop and grow over the last four years.

Lisa Killough-Wells, our office manager, keeps our business running smoothly and has enabled me to gain the time necessary to write this book.

The final acknowledgment goes to my wife, Lorie, who has had a major impact on getting this book produced. As a partner in my business, she provides a level excellence that reflects our company's commitment to quality. As a partner in my life, she supports me when I fall behind, knocks me down when I get too far ahead, and constantly challenges me to be my best.

Table of Contents

About the Author

Work Sheets

Figures

Preface

In most organizations, the normal mode of operation is to drive broad-based change from the top and cascade it down through the ranks. Unfortunately, this is where most organizations fall into the *change trap*. They deploy a large-scale improvement program that has been defined based on reengineering, customer value management, an approach that worked at another company, or one that was touted in such magazines as *Business Week* or the *Harvard Business Review*. When the approach they use to implement change does not match the readiness level of their organization, there is a high probability that the initiative will not meet its proposed objectives. In all likelihood, it will fail.

In *Breaking Out of the Change Trap*, we introduce you to the Organizational Maturity™ change model, which will help you increase your probability for success. It will allow you to realize your long-term goals, while maintaining short-term success. The essence of the Organizational Maturity™ model is:

> To achieve success in any change initiative, the degree and
> level of change must be geared to the level of readiness of the
> organization; if not, there is a mismatch and the initiative is
> destined to fail.

As a leader in today's business environment, you are faced with overwhelming and often conflicting objectives. You must create a vision for the future and deploy an organizational infrastructure that will enable this vision to take shape. At the same time, you need to control the company's visible financial indicators to ensure stability and growth in the markets that you serve.

To attack these two areas concurrently, you must change the way the organization functions. Internally, you need to reevaluate how teams work together, how processes are used and maintained, and how progress and success are measured. Externally, you need to look at the organization's relationships with its customers, with business and economic environments, and with other stakeholders.

As you read this book, you will begin to see how your organization fits into this model of readiness. You will recognize patterns that surround both your successes and failures in trying to drive the organization forward. By sharing this book with members of your staff, you will be able to work as a team to identify the best overall strategy for change based on your readiness level and on the unique needs of your organization.

I wish you the best success on this journey.

Ron Rosenberg
August, 1998

Introduction

Business scenario

The pattern is painfully common. A company is in trouble. It could be because of defective products, poor service, or late deliveries. The impact is clear: customers are irate, employees are frustrated, and management is scrambling to find a solution...fast!

Wanting to do something—needing to do something—the company's senior management team concludes that it needs to change the mode of operation by introducing a new improvement program.

Some cursory research is done into available methods of improvement, and the company begins its change initiative. Someone is appointed the "Change Agent" and is vested with the responsibility for designing, deploying, and implementing this program. Literature is reviewed, other companies are studied, and consultants are contacted. At the conclusion of this exercise, a broad-based improvement program has been defined.

The Change Agent, now working with a "Change Council," develops an introduction and deployment strategy that includes some form of indoctrination for all company employees. Usually this includes an overview of the program and one or more days of training using the featured tool or method on which the program is based.

Teams are formed, employees (already overloaded from "fighting fires") are assigned to work in these teams, and the Change Council sits back and waits for some form of magic to take over. Unfortunately, as time goes on, the demands of the employees' real work takes precedence over participation in the quality-improvement teams. It becomes virtually impossible to get a quorum at meetings, momentum is lost, and employees become cynical—almost disdainful—of the program.

Ultimately, the program loses so much momentum that it literally shuts itself down. Business continues as usual, and the company finds itself in the same position as it was before the program was initiated. Does this sound familiar?

How to break the pattern

If you have responsibility for initiating change in your organization and you want to break this pattern that is all too common in companies today, then you can truly benefit from the information presented in this book. You will learn a comprehensive approach for making tangible improvements in the performance and effectiveness of your organization.

You may be the CEO setting the vision for the company and you want to see what is achievable considering the level of the organization. You may be the person responsible for quality in your organization trying to put into place programs that will help your client groups become more effective. You may be a business owner trying to improve the performance of your business by focusing on improving customer relations. Or you may be a line manager trying to make an impact in your own group to show the rest of the organization that things *can* get better.

You may be the executive responsible for human resource programs to make the organization function more smoothly and effectively. Or you may be in a situation where you are being forced by your manager or customer to do something to address critical performance issues. If you are any one of these individuals trying to initiate change in your company, then you need to see how you can benefit from the information in this book.

How this book will help you

If you are just starting to plan your change initiative, the information here will help you understand how to gauge the readiness level of your organization. Then you can select the deployment approach that will give you the greatest possible chance for success.

If your current program is not getting the kind of results you had hoped for, you will learn how to identify problem areas and how to fine-tune your approach so you can get your program back on track.

If you are already achieving results from your current approach but want to broaden the scope of your influence, you will be able to identify the next steps that will help you take your organization to even greater levels of performance and effectiveness.

How to get the most from this book

This book provides an overview of how your company can benefit by adopting the change strategies described in the following chapters. It will help you determine your group's level of readiness for change, as well as the level of readiness for the organization as a whole. Based on these levels, you will select the approach with the highest probability for success.

It is important to read the chapters in the book in the order presented because they provide a step-by-step model for success. And, by all means, complete the exercises at the end of each chapter. They will enable you to consider and answer difficult questions about the state of your organization. By the time you complete the book, you will have developed a comprehensive documented approach for implementing change.

Your plan for success

As you read the information in this book, look for clues to help you identify your own particular situation. Consider suggestions that make sense for your group and begin to think about what strategies are right for your organization's readiness level for implementing change. Then determine the best ways to apply these strategies to create tangible results in your organization. It will not be as difficult as you might think once you have a plan for success.

Part I

Why Is It So Difficult to Make Change Work?

- Chapter 1—How to Begin Your Journey for Change

- Chapter 2—Characteristics of Empowered Cultures

- Chapter 3—Roadblocks to Success

1

How to Begin Your Journey for Change

No one approach to organizational change is best

If there was only one approach to organizational change that worked best of all, then there would be little confusion about which method to choose. But organizations *are* different, and they each have different needs. What works in one situation may not work in another.

When I started training in the martial arts in 1980, a question frequently asked during our belt promotions was, "What is the *best* style of martial arts?" As our style was an Okinawan style called "Isshin Ryu," many people answered "Isshin Ryu."

Of course, this answer was wrong. As our instructor explained, if any one style were truly best, truly universal, and truly applicable in all situations, it alone would have survived, unchallenged, and unchanged for thousands of years—and all other styles would have faded. In fact, there are hundreds of styles of martial arts and many branches within each of these individual styles. It is a matter of finding the style that is best for you.

The same is true for the various styles of organizational improvement. No one approach works in all situations, for all organizations, or for all issues. It is essential to identify an approach that will work for *your* particular organization!

Focus on the content, not on the acronyms

The different approaches to organizational change—Malcolm Baldrige, ISO 9000, Reengineering, Customer Value Management, Employee Satisfaction, and 360° Feedback—are all useful in certain circumstances. Although they seem vastly different on the surface, most improvement methods are more alike than they are different.

3

The concepts of respect for people, management by fact and data, continuous improvement, and customer focus have been present in business approaches used by successful organizations for many, many years and will be present for many more.

This book does not go into the details of any specific approach—there are many excellent sources of information in this area, and it is not the main focus of this model.

This book *will* help to identify the best approach for your group based on your current situation, the best scope for effective deployment, and the best way to position this effort to get the highest level of support from your own team and from your management.

Exercise—Identify your current environment

To reach a destination, it is always helpful to know where you are when you start out. The following areas are critical to understanding the makeup of an organization that wants to be successful.

On **Work Sheet 1**, **page 6**, describe your current situation as it relates to the following characteristics.

Organization Type: Many problems are common to all types of organizations, but there are some issues which are endemic to specific organization types. Are you a public-sector group, an educational institution, or a commercial or high-tech corporation?

Group
Characteristics: Define the group over which you have some direct influence. How large is it? What types of positions do the individuals in your group possess: professional, technical, manufacturing, administrative, clerical, or management? As we go through the model, this is the group that will be used to target your change initiative.

Parent Organization: In most cases, your group is part of a larger organization. It may be the department to which your team reports. Or your department may report to a larger organization. Or your division may report to a larger corporate entity. In any case, the relationship between your group and the parent organization will have a major impact on your deployment approach.

Purpose:

Why does your group exist? What critical outputs would disappear if your group's function was eliminated? Understanding the purpose your group serves is essential as you begin to select an improvement strategy that will match your needs.

Customers:

Do you know who your customers are? Your external customers are the ones that your company, institution, or agency serves and, in most cases, they are the revenue source for your organization. What about internal customers? Is the relationship between you and your internal customers a *partnership*? Instead of groups inside the organization serving other groups, try to think of this relationship as *teaming*; that is, groups working together with the common goal of serving the external customer.

Customer Values:

Once customers have been identified, take a minute to try to understand what is important to them and how this data can be measured. Do your customers value quick turnaround, high quality, or lots of features and services? It could be all three. Try to list some examples of what your customers value, what their expectations are, and how these expectations are identified and measured.

Suppliers:

It is virtually impossible to create a product or deliver a service in a vacuum. All groups have inputs—whether tangible or intangible—which help to produce the final product. What materials, information, or other inputs does your group need to be successful in this endeavor?

Work Sheet 1—Current Environment

Instructions: Describe your current organizational environment as related to the characteristics on **pages 4** and **5**.

Organization Type: _____

Group Characteristics: _____

Parent Organization: _____

Purpose: _____

_____

_____

_____

Customers: _____

_____

_____

_____

Customer Values: _____

_____

_____

_____

Suppliers: _____

_____

_____

_____

_____

Exercise—Identify your current change initiatives

As we work together to improve the overall effectiveness of your change initiative, it is important to understand exactly where your efforts stand right now.

On **Work Sheet 2**, **page 8** describe the situation in which your organization finds itself in these areas.

Current Initiatives:

What change initiatives is your organization currently involved in? These may be formal quality approaches like Malcolm Baldrige, ISO 9000, QS 9000, or the SEI Capability Maturity Model. They could also be directed towards other areas like team building, empowerment, or communications.

Status:

Next, and more importantly, how are these efforts working? Are they being supported by the people in your group? By your leadership team? Are the efforts producing tangible business results that add value to the organization?

Past Initiatives:

What similar types of programs have you had in your organization in the past?

Status:

Were they successful? If they were, what made them work for you? If they were not, what do you think caused them to deliver less than you had hoped?

Roadblocks:

What has interfered with your plans? The answer could include budgetary constraints, transition in your organization's leadership, downsizing, aggressive development and delivery deadlines, economic considerations, or a combination of some or all of these roadblocks!

Work Sheet 2—Current Efforts

Instructions: Describe your organization's current efforts as related to the characteristics on **page 7**.

Current Initiatives: _____

_____

_____

_____

Status: _____

_____

_____

_____

Past Initiatives: _____

_____

_____

_____

Status: _____

_____

_____

_____

Roadblocks: _____

_____

_____

_____

2

Characteristics of Empowered Cultures

Five characteristics of successful organizations

To create an environment where change is not only possible, but is also an accepted part of the culture, it is necessary to first look at the characteristics that embody this type of company. Companies are at various levels of readiness for change. The level determines the extent to which an organization can make fundamental changes in the way it operates the business.

When we do workshops with senior leadership teams, we frequently ask them what they believe are the characteristics of successful organizations. Companies which possess these characteristics have the ability to respond effectively to change and embrace the challenges it creates. Without exception, the five areas listed below are identified among the responses.

These five characteristics are extremely important in helping to create an environment in which a customer-focused, improvement-driven mindset is the norm. As each one is discussed, it will become apparent how critical it is to implementing successful change.

1. Vision Alignment

A clear vision of a company's direction and goals allows employees to make decisions that are consistent with a higher purpose and not just what the management, market, or product flavor of the month happens to be.

It also allows groups to work together more cooperatively because they are working toward a common goal instead of supporting "warring fiefdoms." And because there is a clear vision of where the organization is headed, it makes long-term planning easier and much more valid.

In the absence of a documented, communicated vision, the only place where this perspective occurs is at the senior management level. When this happens, it is difficult to start a program because it may not be in line with the CEO's vision for the company. Also, it may only address one component of the organization's needs. Similarly, a loosely defined vision allows different groups to move in conflicting directions while they may believe they are working cooperatively.

2. Management Involvement

Management involvement is a key component because employees are more convinced by a manager's actions than by his or her words. The people in the group learn what the organization values by seeing how managers spend their time and energy, not by any highlights they may jot down on an overhead at the weekly staff meeting.

A leader may try to delegate responsibility for change initiatives, but this usually does not work. Even though the delegate is operating with implied authority, other people in the organization may look for opportunities to continue business as usual—and they will probably get conflicting signals from their leadership about priorities.

If the leader spends her time in a business as usual mode, she can bet everyone else in the group will do the same. Leading by example is always the most effective way to get the behavior you want from your team.

3. Employee Empowerment

Most good managers know that the people closest to the work have the best knowledge of what it takes to do the work. The role leadership should play to empower its employees is to set the direction and lead by example.

The best results are often seen when organizations reward and encourage innovation. High-performance groups learn to recognize the capabilities of their employees. This allows the organization to provide an appropriate level of freedom, autonomy, and responsibility which leads to improved teamwork and greater focus on the mission of the company.

When employees continually make valid suggestions on how to improve the work process, but are routinely stopped in their tracks by the leadership, employees become frustrated and eventually give up and stop trying.

4. Customer Focus

It is important to emphasize that an organization exists to serve its customers. Everything else supports this primary purpose. At times, there may be several groups of customers which have competing needs. As a result, it is necessary to look closely at how to accommodate and reconcile the various needs of this diverse group of customers to ensure their satisfaction.

A common principle is that people move towards pleasure and away from pain. If a company offers poor quality products and services to its customers, they will avoid it at all costs. They will, on the other hand, show extreme loyalty to a company which offers superior products and services. This principle should be of utmost importance when establishing guidelines for customer interaction.

5. Process Base

A strong process base is the foundation on which all improvement is built and is a critical component in the success of organizations.

Many organizations focus so much on process that they end up serving the process instead of the other way around. But many others suffer from a complete lack of process. They do not have a method in place to repeat their successes or correct their failures. To ensure that companies are able to benefit from their experiences, they need to incorporate a strong process foundation into the workings of their organization.

All organizations are unique

Every organization has its own unique strengths and weaknesses. One company may be very focused on the customer, but lack a standard process base to ensure that customer issues are handled consistently and fairly. Another company may have a clear vision of the company's direction, yet its management sends mixed messages to employees.

Managers may say they are committed to the vision; however, their actions and the work they focus on are incongruent with the mission of the company. To help determine where an organization currently stands, it is necessary to look at each area objectively.

Exercise—Strengths and Weaknesses

On **page 12**, there is a list of these five areas of excellence along with two columns in which to record strengths and weaknesses. For each area, list the strengths and weaknesses that pertain to your group as well as those which are present in your organization as a whole. This will give you a realistic view of exactly where your organization stands currently.

Work Sheet 3—Strengths and Weaknesses

Instructions: Describe the strengths and weaknesses of your group and organization as related to the characteristics discussed on **pages 9-11**.

Area	Strengths	Weaknesses
1. Vision Alignment:	_____	_____
	_____	_____
	_____	_____
	_____	_____
2. Management Involvement:	_____	_____
	_____	_____
	_____	_____
	_____	_____
3. Employee Empowerment:	_____	_____
	_____	_____
	_____	_____
	_____	_____
4. Customer Focus:	_____	_____
	_____	_____
	_____	_____
	_____	_____
5. Process Base:	_____	_____
	_____	_____
	_____	_____
	_____	_____

3

Roadblocks to Success

If we know where to go, why is change so difficult?

When trying to assimilate the five major characteristics of empowered cultures listed in **Chapter 2**, it is necessary for companies to overcome a variety of obstacles that may hinder their efforts to achieve successful change. These roadblocks are as diverse as the companies they come from.

The following roadblocks are representative of some of the issues individuals are facing today when trying to implement organizational change. As you read each of the descriptions, decide if the roadblock is affecting your progress. Later on in **Part 4** we discuss specific approaches to help you address these roadblocks as you attempt to implement change.

Roadblock: A group that reports to someone else

It is very difficult to be responsible for improvement initiatives for a group that does not directly report to you. Even if you have the best intentions, the group may perceive that you are interfering where you do not belong. As an outsider, you appear to know little about the real issues and how they can best be solved. This will make it difficult for you to gain support from the group.

Roadblock: Without support there can be no change

Among people with functions like corporate quality director, change agent, and vice president of human resources there is a great debate over the *best* way to achieve significant results from change initiatives.

One widely held belief is that to achieve tangible change, the support of senior management is needed. This belief makes sense for a variety of reasons and is frequently used as a lever to get senior managers on board. Just as frequently, however, it is used as justification by middle managers to abdicate responsibility for ownership of their functions or as an excuse for a well-intentioned—but unsuccessful—change initiative.

The important thing to keep in perspective is that while it is important to have senior leadership support, *how* you define senior leadership makes the difference between success and failure. Leadership occurs at many levels, and similarly, change can occur at many levels.

Roadblock: Function versus process organization

Many organizations still face the problem that they are organized along silo-like functions, instead of along cross-functional lines. These groups are focused solely on their own functional area without any interaction with the groups that are upstream or downstream in the overall process.

This type of organization prevents individual groups from playing a part in the end-to-end processes that directly serve the customer base. This traditional, hierarchical system can promote a culture in which competing groups battle against each other—sometimes for the sake of competition—instead of working together to initiate improvement efforts that will meet the needs and expectations of their customers.

Roadblock: Rewards based on individual versus team performance

From the time we entered kindergarten, through high school and college, the instructions were always the same: keep your eyes on your own paper; do your own assignment; do not get help from your friends.

When we start our careers, eager to make an impact, we are told about the importance of working in teams. Although this is contradictory to everything we have been taught up to this point, it somehow makes sense, so we become hopeful and optimistic.

Unfortunately, this euphoria is short-lived. In most organizations, when it comes time for compensation and recognition, everything is based on individual—not team—performance. How can we expect people to invest the effort and energy that are needed in a team environment when we reward them based on the success of their individual efforts?

Roadblock: Rewards based on short-term performance

At lower levels in an organization—the levels where the more noticeable work actually takes place—it is appropriate for performance to be measured on short-term accomplishment: closing the books at the end of the period, correcting a missed shipment, or completing a development project on time.

Unfortunately, this short-term mentality frequently remains with managers as they progress farther and farther up the ladder. This situation is further aggravated by the fact that, in many organizations, short-term efforts are the only ones that are routinely rewarded.

This makes for an extremely difficult environment in which to attempt change because many approaches to change and improvement require an investment of funds, resources, and *time*. If the organization is too focused on short-term outcomes, it will be virtually impossible to gain the commitment necessary to make significant and lasting change.

Roadblock: Rewarding effort instead of results

A surprising number of organizations reward effort rather than results. For example, the raise, bonus, and promotion, as well as the glory may go to the employee who successfully deals with a major customer crisis— *even if he was the one who caused it in the first place!*

The way to determine an organization's values —its *real* values which may or may not be the same ones posted on the wall in the boardroom—is to look at who gets rewarded and take note of that person's activities.

Roadblock: Change blockers

In almost every organization, as in most personal situations, there are some people who will resist change. They may simply be apprehensive about an unknown future. They may be comfortable with the status quo. Or they may have a vested interest in keeping things the way they are. It may also be the fact that people tend to be naturally resistant to change. For whatever reason, these individuals who resist change will have a negative impact and will seriously impede the organization's efforts to change.

Roadblock: The "do more with less" approach

Frequently, organizations reduce staffing to minimum levels and expect employees to produce the same level of output. This *do more with less* approach burns people out so that they do not have the energy to attack improvement with the level of enthusiasm that is needed.

Too often, we form unreasonable expectations about what our teams are capable of and then expect them to fulfill these expectations. Often, the managers in these organizations do not realize that they have pushed their people too far. I have a very clear recollection early in my career of a director of engineering telling our team that it was okay to burn out engineers. You can see how this would demoralize even the most enthusiastic group.

Roadblock: No training—just get better!

Sometimes, the organization takes a more severe approach to change. There is no training, no investment in resources, and no commitment of time. There is only a mandate to "Do better!" Curiously, these organizations, when confronted with employees' perceptions of this situation, will insist that this is a *work smarter—not harder* approach, not the *do more with less* approach that it generally is.

Roadblock: Too busy

"I'm too busy," can be a valid explanation for deferring a change initiative. There can be a sudden burst of sales that requires the focus of everyone involved. Or there might be an important market opportunity that requires immediate attention.

The problem is that very often, as in our personal lives, the things that people are too busy with are often not really important—just *urgent*. A flurry of activity can make us feel like we are really contributing to the success of the company.

If, however, there are major changes that need to be addressed and everyone is too busy to get to them, then the activities that could really help the organization are ignored and never fully addressed.

Roadblock: There is not enough money in the budget

Organizations in the early stages of maturity tend to operate more from a tactical approach rather than from a strategic approach. This often means that decisions about investing in new programs, methodologies, tools, and training are made more often because of budgetary issues rather than by the actual needs of the organization.

Many organizations seem to run out of money, with frightening predictability, at the same time every year and put into place across-the-board cost-cutting measures like travel, hiring, and training freezes.

This seasonal approach to spending can have a dramatic impact on change and improvement initiatives because the best-laid plans will lose momentum and come to a grinding halt. When funding is cut, the attention of employees will be diverted back to the real world crisis mode.

Roadblock: Change as an event—not a process

Change initiatives frequently happen in response to a major crisis. For example, a serious situation may arise in which a customer threatens action if the situation is not remedied quickly. Special teams are formed with key employees who must identify the problem and fix the root cause. Unfortunately, when the immediate crisis is solved, it is back to business as usual. For change to be effective, it must be sustainable, not a discrete event.

Roadblock: Success

One of the most potent roadblocks to change is success! People in several companies have complained, "We really need to improve in the 'X' area, but we are so successful that we cannot get anyone's attention."

Why do they need to change if they are so successful? The answer invariably is that the success may be a result of a lack of competition or a limited market advantage. If the company does not start making improvements now, it could be left behind when the environment changes and the company cannot match the competition.

Roadblock: Flavor of the month approach with competing initiatives

Many times, a major roadblock to successful change is an organization's previous attempts at change. Although usually done with the best of intentions, too many groups roll out one improvement model after another in a seemingly endless sequence.

This *flavor of the month* approach only makes people more and more cynical over time. Besides the actual failure of the initiative, a failed rollout almost always discourages future attempts at change.

Roadblock: Premature training

In an attempt to get everyone involved, and under the good intention of "establishing a common language" or "defining a common process," many organizations try to launch their change initiatives by putting all employees through a standardized training program.

Unfortunately, if the organization is not at a high enough level of readiness, this approach can be a huge waste of time, energy, and resources. Typically, the effectiveness of change programs deployed under this approach is measured by the number of people trained and the number of teams formed. Unfortunately, most people in the organization will recognize that these metrics are meaningless.

Roadblock: Fear of working oneself out of a job

Some of the reluctance towards improvement and change initiatives comes from a fear of being so successful that one will actually work oneself out of a job. In many cases, this is an unfounded fear. Individuals who can effect change in an organization are in high demand these days—both inside and outside their own organization.

Unfortunately, in many cases, reengineering has become a euphemism for downsizing. Organizations have reengineered employees out of their jobs. In many cases, this was necessary. But there continue to be stories of cases where this was just a facade for cuts that were already planned.

Roadblock: It will never work here—our organization is different

Businesses have the constant pressures of product deadlines, bottom-line results, regulatory issues, and increasing competition. One would expect that addressing these issues would drive companies to find ways to become more efficient and effective, but often they become paralyzed to the point where they do nothing but flounder.

And this is not limited to the corporate environment. Educational institutions have their own set of issues. Budget cuts, changing requirements and needs, and alternative approaches to traditional methods keep things in a constant state of flux.

In the public sector, staffing levels—right down to the individual position—are frequently set by state or local legislators. The entire leadership of the organization is potentially changed every few years, meaning that any progress that has been made may be lost.

Whenever a cookie-cutter approach to improvement is introduced, there are always the naysayers who claim that, "It won't work here because our organization is different." And it is hard to separate the resistance from the truth. Some people in an organization look for any excuse to dismiss an effort that will require them to change their behavior.

There is a lot of validity in saying that a *one-size-fits-all* approach to change will not work. In fact, that is the whole point. You need to tailor your approach to change to meet the needs of your organization.

It is time to make change happen

If you are trying to make improvements in your organization, it may seem as if you are trying to move a large object by tying a rope to it and pushing on the rope. It gets really frustrating, and brings to mind an apt statement: "The only good thing about banging your head against the wall is that it feels good when you stop."

So, stop banging your head against the wall. Recognize that change is difficult. Recognize that you will not always get the level of support you want—or need. On the brighter side, recognize that step-by-step you *can* begin to make progress in your change efforts by understanding the capability of your organization to support its change initiatives.

What is important for you to remember is that organizations at *all* levels of readiness can successfully initiate change—it is simply a matter of doing the following.

- Identify the level of readiness and select an appropriate approach to implementing change.

- Recognize that in the real world, change usually happens from the inside out, not from the top down.

Exercise—Roadblocks to Change

On **page 20**, list the roadblocks to change in your organization. You may find that your organization has some of the issues discussed already, and it is likely that you have a few more that are directly related to your group's history and culture.

By writing them down, you will have the opportunity to review them. Then you can consider how they are impacting your efforts to change.

Work Sheet 4—Roadblocks to Change

Instructions: Describe the roadblocks you have experienced in your organization when trying to implement change.

1. _____

_____

_____

2. _____

_____

_____

3. _____

_____

_____

4. _____

_____

_____

5. _____

_____

_____

6. _____

_____

_____

7. _____

_____

_____

Part 2

The Organizational Maturity™ Model

- Chapter 4—The Concept of Organizational Maturity™

- Chapter 5—Firefighting Level

- Chapter 6—Emerging Level

- Chapter 7—Total Commitment Level

- Chapter 8—Understanding the Levels of Organizational Maturity™

4

The Concept of Organizational Maturity™

Organizations are at varying levels of readiness for change

One of the most important concepts to understand when trying to implement change is that organizations are at different levels of readiness for change. And within a particular organization, different groups are at different levels of readiness for change. This may seem like a childishly obvious thing to say. But while many people recognize the validity of this statement intellectually, they fail to apply it practically.

It is important to determine your group's readiness level *before* implementing a change initiative or the results could be disastrous, even deadly as we can see from the following example.

Scenario

You wake up in the morning with a sharp, intense pain in your chest and numbness down your arm. You make an appointment with the doctor right away and the conversation goes somewhat like this.

You: Doctor, I have this sharp pain right here, and...

Doctor: Stop! Don't say another word; I know what the problem is. You have gastritis. Take several doses of an antacid for the next few days and let me know how you feel. That will be $75; you can pay out front, and have a nice day!

Did you feel a little uncomfortable about the situation? Note that the physician did not really ask any questions. He did not listen completely to the symptoms. Yet he went ahead and prescribed an antacid.

What is wrong with this scenario?

First, your symptoms could have been caused by a peptic ulcer or, even worse, you may have been exhibiting the symptoms of a heart attack.

The bottom line is that the doctor failed to do one of the most important functions in all of medicine: he did not perform a proper diagnosis.

If this were your situation, you would probably be upset. You would most likely stop the doctor and try to provide some additional information, or, at least, ask some more questions. You might even go so far as to report the doctor to the state licensing board.

In the medical profession, proper diagnosis is a major part of a physician's job. To make an accurate diagnosis of a patient's illness, a doctor must take adequate time to assess the symptoms to determine a proper treatment plan. If his treatment plan does not match the symptoms, the results could be disastrous. In the most extreme case, the result could be fatal.

Diagnose the business environment

Unlike most medical situations, where an accurate diagnosis is imperative, organizations are not as concerned with performing a proper analysis of their business environment before selecting and committing to major change initiatives. They fail to assess their overall level of readiness to see how this will impact their change efforts.

Deciding to overhaul the compensation scheme, undertaking a major change initiative, or applying for a national quality award without looking first at the organization is exactly the same as prescribing medical treatment without first understanding the symptoms.

In business, as well as in the medical field, you first need to make a proper diagnosis of the particular situation or environment before you proceed with a treatment plan. Your probability for success is much greater when you take this approach.

Organizational Maturity™ model

While there may be varying degrees of readiness for change, it is useful to identify and refer to the three primary ranges on the readiness scale.

The Organizational Maturity™ model defines an organization's environment in terms of its readiness for change. The three primary levels in the model are *Firefighting, Emerging*, and *Total Commitment*.

Figure 1 on **page 25** provides a high-level overview of each level as it relates to the five characteristics of high-performance organizations. You

Figure 1—Levels of Readiness versus Five Characteristics

Characteristics	Readiness Levels		
	Firefighting	Emerging	Total Commitment
1. **Vision**	Unclear	Scattered	Clear
2. **Management Involvement**	Authoritarian	Transitional	Role Model
3. **Employee Empowerment**	None	Limited	Active
4. **Customer Focus**	Reactive	Participative	Partnering
5. **Process Base**	None	Ad hoc	Process Management

may notice that it is common for an organization to be at the Firefighting level in one area, but at the Emerging level in another. As you will see, however, there is usually a concentration in one of the readiness levels that defines the organization's overall level of readiness.

The Organizational Maturity™ model is designed to allow you to perform a diagnosis of your organization's readiness for change and to guide you in selecting an approach for change that will have the greatest possible chance for success.

The next three chapters introduce the three levels of Organizational Maturity™, the needs of organizations at each level, and the consequences of mismatching approach and readiness.

In **Chapter 19**, you will perform a unique self-assessment that will bring you new understanding into why your current initiatives are producing disappointing results or will help you move forward if you are just beginning.

5

Firefighting Level

Constantly putting out fires

A Firefighting organization functions just like the name implies. The organization is so busy putting out fires that it has no time for planning and developing consistent policies. Each day employees react to the problems that constantly arise in their group, so that the only consistency is that they will run from one fire to the next. Five characteristics of a Firefighting organization follow.

1. Unclear vision

In a Firefighting organization, vision is unclear because the organization either never took the time to develop a clear sense of direction or because it got so caught up in a reactive mode that it completely lost sight of its mission. In either case, when the vision is unclear, members of the organization do not always see where the company is going.

2. Authoritarian management style

The management style in this type of organization will tend to be old-style authoritarian, such as, "If I want your opinion, I'll give it to you!" The reason for this is that when you are in a Firefighting mode, you have to constantly direct your staff to perform specific tasks.

Imagine an actual fire crew arriving at the scene of a raging fire. The fire captain does not invite the firefighters to form a continuous improvement team to determine the best approach to putting out the fire—he just barks out orders: "Jones! Get the hose hooked up!" "Martinez! Get the ladder out!" This same type of thing happens in Firefighting organizations on a daily basis.

3. Lack of employee empowerment

Most companies have a list of core beliefs or values which they try to communicate to all employees. Most of these contain some reference to people. For instance, "Our people are our greatest asset." Or, "Our employees make us number one!" Unfortunately, when these same employees make suggestions about ways to improve, they are often met with resistance, confrontation, or indifference.

4. Reactive customer service

The relationship with the customer will be a very sensitive issue. When problems arise, the organization will usually fix them quickly. When the exact same problems appear with a different customer, they will be fixed again. The process will be repeated many times. However, no one will take the time to identify and address the root causes that allowed the problems to occur in the first place.

5. Lack of process

Finally, the Firefighting organization will tend to suffer from a lack of process. If things are working well, there will be no guarantee of repeating the success. When problems appear—even if the root causes are identified—there will be no way to make the improvements a permanent part of the work process because the organization lacks a well understood, documented process to guide the group. And even if the process is formally documented, it may not be followed. Often, the informal *street process* is the actual method used.

6

Emerging Level

Progressive versus business-as-usual environment

The identifying characteristic of the Emerging organization is that some groups are ready to move forward while others are stuck in the status quo. This presents a unique opportunity for groups that are ready to change to set the example for the rest of the organization. Five characteristics of an Emerging organization follow.

1. Scattered vision

Vision in the Emerging organization really depends on what part of the organization you look at. In the groups that are moving forward, there will be a well-defined and well-understood sense of direction. In other parts of the organization there will be the same kind of vision as in the Firefighting groups: either no clear direction or one that is out of date or out of style.

2. Transitional management involvement

In management involvement, there is the same kind of split as indicated in scattered vision above. The more progressive groups will have an involved set of leaders who model the activities and behaviors that will move the group ahead. In other groups, frustration will be evident as less effective managers struggle between the behavior they would like to demonstrate and the behavior they exhibit because of the firefighting conditions.

In either case, any successes a manager achieves will be transitional. If the manager moves to another group, the progress she has made will go with her to the new group, allowing her former group to return to its old patterns of behavior. Change in this type of environment is typically tied to the manager and not to the group's systematic approach.

3. Limited employee input

As employees try to become more active and help improve the work situation, the best results will come from the forward-thinking groups where employee input is not only accepted but is also encouraged. In other parts of the organization, there may be some progress in getting input from lower levels; but, more often than not, groups will continue to run into roadblocks including no time, no money, and no resources.

4. Participative customer relationship

In the Emerging organization there are higher levels of customer involvement than at the Firefighting level. When trying to solve problems, the organization will seek participation from customer groups to address their issues of concern and to identify the root causes to prevent future problems from occurring. There will be a lot more communication with customers to inform them about improvement activities and share the results of performance and customer satisfaction initiatives.

5. Ad hoc process management

Finally, a growing awareness of the importance of process management is evident in the Emerging organization, though decidedly ad hoc in many groups. This is the phase where many groups begin to realize that a systematic approach to process management can actually help them be more effective in producing products and providing services. And it can also help them be more responsive to their customers.

Total Commitment Level

Organized, focused, and committed

The Total Commitment organization is the one everyone would probably like to work in because it is organized and focused. It successfully demonstrates the characteristics that define an empowered culture: vision alignment, management involvement, employee empowerment, customer focus, and process base. Five characteristics of a Total Commitment organization follow.

1. Clear direction

In the Total Commitment organization, the short- and long-term direction is clear and, more importantly, is communicated effectively throughout the organization. This enables everyone to understand the high-level direction for the organization and exactly how these objectives will be achieved over the coming years.

2. Leadership by example

What makes these organizations exciting is that the vision is communicated not only by actions, but also by *behaviors*. Leaders in the company model the values of the organization in their interactions with employees, customers, and the community at large.

When a change initiative is introduced into the company, these leaders will frequently set the example by applying the new approach to their own management systems before asking others in the organization to do the same in their own functions.

When people spend time on an activity, it sends a message that the activity is important to them.

3. Active employee participation

In the Total Commitment scenario, employees have a greater say in what goes on in the organization, resulting in a more enjoyable environment.

There is an incredible amount of flexibility given to managers and individual contributors because of the high degree of alignment around a clear vision. People who work in this kind of organization do not have to choose between believing what the manager says and what he does because there is no difference between the two.

The opportunity for empowerment and self-direction is greatest in the Total Commitment organization. When mission and values are clearly communicated, employees are able to take risks and be innovative because they know that they are acting in the best interests of the organization.

4. Partnering with customers

The Total Commitment organization provides a unique framework for customer interaction. Customers are frequently involved as partners not only in solving problems, but also in participating in product development and in the definition of services.

Organizations at other levels that are not comfortable with their internal workings cannot possibly be secure enough to allow this kind of customer participation to take place.

Total Commitment organizations, in contrast, will have honed their own internal operations to such a high level that this kind of customer involvement will be effective and appropriate.

5. Strong process management

The only way to maintain performance at this high level is to have a set of systematic and repeatable processes in place, which are continually improved upon based on root cause data, employee input, and customer feedback. In these organizations, process owners are clearly identified, and specific measures are used to help improve the processes.

Organizations at the Total Commitment level have established formal methods to introduce and manage processes that help support their objectives. In these organizations, the processes are there to serve the employees so that they can service their customers more effectively.

8

Understanding the Levels of Organizational Maturity™

Identify the characteristics at each readiness level

To begin to apply the model of Organizational Maturity™, it is necessary to first become familiar with the characteristics of organizations at all three levels of readiness. The model can be applied to all types of organizations from public sector groups to educational institutions and from small businesses to high-tech corporations. The following three examples will help you recognize the differences in these levels.

1. Firefighting scenario

Consider the case of a state agency where constant contact with its customers is the main function.

This agency has been receiving complaints about poor service, inaccurate mailings, and extremely slow response to inquiries. In fact, some customers have been so enraged that they have begun contacting their state legislators to voice their feelings at a time when the legislature is already considering cutting the agency's funding as part of a broad budget reduction effort.

Look at the characteristics of this group: the mission statement is at least twenty-five years old and is ignored by most people in the group who consider it outdated and irrelevant. There is no alignment or sense of purpose to help drive people's behavior.

The leadership of this group seems more interested in protecting its jobs than in identifying and fixing the problems it faces.

Employees feel trapped in a situation in which they have no input and no impact, and their frustration shows in their attitude towards customers, whom they consider to be adversaries and nuisances.

The processes they follow are well-defined, but are so inflexible that they limit the employees' ability to serve their customers.

2. Emerging scenario

A 1,000-person division of a large corporation has both vision and mission statements, but they are not widely embraced. Management has rolled out a major quality program, but it has balked at implementing many of the suggested improvements because of a lack of funds and time to adequately staff the efforts. Employees are becoming frustrated at this approach.

Major customers are beginning to call more frequently to complain about product defects. "You get the problems turned around fast enough, but they keep happening!" they say. "If the rest of your organization worked as well as the Customer Response team, we'd be ecstatic."

Employees have complained that the company's policies and procedures are laughable and that the processes they are supposed to follow are extremely outdated and do not resemble the processes they are actually using on a daily basis.

This is all characteristic of an Emerging group. The vision exists, but it is shaky. Management is inconsistent in its support of improvement activities, and employees clearly recognize this.

The customer interface is somewhere between reactive and participative; and, though an attempt has been made at managing processes, the results are decidedly ad hoc.

3. Total Commitment scenario

A small local college is in the Total Commitment phase. The college began to plan for the future with a series of strategic planning sessions. It identified the long-term mission. Then it created a set of values that would help guide it as it began to determine the direction of its long-term mission.

As part of this effort, a set of actions was developed, which would be addressed by teams made up of the college's senior leadership team and a selected group of motivated staff members and instructors.

This first set of actions had been completed and resulted in key processes being defined in a number of important areas. A separate effort, which involved extensive interviews and focus groups, gave a clear understanding of the customer base and the expectations of these customers.

Because of these efforts, the college was ready to begin the next phase in the evolution, which was a more broad-based approach to improvement.

Exercise—Level of Organizational Maturity™

In order to get a general sense of where the company or larger organization—of which your group is a part—fits in the three levels of Organizational Maturity™, look at **Work Sheet 5** on **page 36**. The indicators for each of the five characteristics of high-performance organizations are broken out by readiness levels.

Take a few minutes to think about where your organization falls in each of these five areas. Then circle in the appropriate column the indicator that corresponds to your level of readiness.

For example, if your organization has processes that are defined but not widely followed, circle "Ad hoc." If your leadership tends to be more transitional than authoritarian, circle "Transitional."

This chart will give you a general idea of your organization's level of readiness for change. Later on, you will go through a more detailed assessment of your level of Organizational Maturity™ to pinpoint both your group's and your organization's levels of readiness for change.

Work Sheet 5—Level of Organizational Maturity™

Instructions: Review the table below and circle in the appropriate column the indicator that corresponds to the level of readiness of your company or organization.

	Readiness Levels		
Characteristics	**Firefighting**	**Emerging**	**Total Commitment**
1. **Vision**	Unclear	Scattered	Clear
2. **Management Involvement**	Authoritarian	Transitional	Role Model
3. **Employee Empowerment**	None	Limited	Active
4. **Customer Focus**	Reactive	Participative	Partnering
5. **Process Base**	None	Ad hoc	Process Management

Part 3

Selecting the
Right Approach

◆ Chapter 9—Needs and Approaches for Each Level

◆ Chapter 10—The Impact of Mismatching Approach and Readiness

9

Needs and Approaches
for Each Level

With accurate diagnosis, the solution is easy

As we discussed previously, a large part of a physician's work involves diagnosis. Once the problem has been determined, the treatment is usually pretty straightforward. This approach is similar to prescribing a treatment plan for an organization that may or may not be in a healthy state.

The key is to correctly diagnose an organization's level of readiness in order to identify the approach that will more closely match the particular needs of this organization.

Scenario

In **Chapter 4**, we gave an example of a person visiting a doctor with chest pains and being prescribed treatment for gastritis. Because the proper diagnosis was not really made, it was never clear if that was actually the patient's true problem.

In fact, after taking several doses of an antacid, the patient continues to experience pressure in his chest, numbness down his arm, and sweating. He decides to go to the hospital because the symptoms seem to be getting worse. Suddenly, he clutches his chest, loses his balance, and falls quickly to the floor.

How would you help in this situation?

- Take a medical history?
- Phone 911 and begin administering CPR?
- Explain to him that by managing his stress level, physical fitness, and dietary habits he might have been able to prevent this unfortunate situation?

The most logical choice would be to phone 911 and administer CPR. The patient is not breathing, and his heart has stopped. He needs immediate intervention to help him survive the heart attack. The other options are appropriate for follow-up and would almost certainly be necessary for a full recovery.

Obviously, suggesting an exercise program to a patient in the middle of a heart attack would be ridiculous based on his life-threatening needs. Likewise, it is useless to implement broad-based change to an organization which is at the Firefighting level.

Organizations at different levels of readiness have different needs. This concept is summarized in **Figure 2**. Each case describes the needs of the organization, the goal of the initiative, and the type of approach that will have the highest probability for success.

Figure 2—Needs of the Organization

Readiness Levels	Needs	Goals	Approach
Firefighting	Survival	Stability	Problem-solving
Emerging	Healing	Mobilization	Focused Change
Total Commitment	Change of Lifestyle	World Class Performance	Broad-based Change

Problem-solving approach in Firefighting organizations

A Firefighting organization has a variety of issues that need to be addressed on a long-term basis. However, the immediate need is to survive. The goal is to stabilize the organization so that long-term actions can be initiated. The way to accomplish this is by using a *problem-solving* approach to change.

Problem-solving approaches are very basic techniques which are focused on solving specific issues. Examples might include analyzing defect data or identifying corrective actions for highly visible errors.

Once you understand the organization's immediate problems, you can address its most critical issues. Do whatever it takes to *stabilize* the organization so that the larger systemic problems can be addressed.

"Wait a minute!" you say, "That doesn't sound like *top-down-cascaded-through-the-organization* change. That doesn't sound like *reengineering*." No it does not. And this is important because the group is not ready for anything that complex. It would surely fail as we will see in **Chapter 10**.

This type of environment is similar to being in a small rowboat out in the middle of a lake. Suddenly a huge gaping hole appears in the rowboat! Water gushes into the boat almost as fast as you can bail it out. *Yes*, you have to patch up the hole. *Yes*, you want to know how it happened so you can prevent it in the future. But all you can do right *now* is bail water out of the boat or it will sink. Your only concern is getting back to shore safely.

It is interesting that organizations, like individuals, do not always recognize that they are in the Firefighting stage until something tragic happens. Just as there are people with cholesterol levels over 300, blood pressure of 180/120, and enough stress to stop a train, there are organizations that are in the same walking time bomb mode and *do not even know it!*

Organizations frequently dismiss high attrition, illness, and other similar conditions as simply *characteristic of our particular industry* when these may, in fact, be early-warning signs of impending problems.

Focused change approach in Emerging organizations

Let us take another look at the heart-attack victim mentioned earlier. At the hospital, the staff may run some tests, monitor his condition, prescribe medication, or perhaps even perform surgery. They help the patient by focusing on the cause of the problem and treating it specifically. This is the same approach that should be used in Emerging organizations.

First, you need to select the most important area to address and determine what can be done to improve the situation. Decide how progress will be measured, and then proceed with your change initiative.

The goal is to mobilize the organization so it is prepared to make broader changes that will have a greater impact on the organization and take the company to the next level.

It is important to select only one issue to work on at a time and narrow the scope of the action. The problem many organizations run into is that they try to fix everything at once. This rarely works in the best of circumstances and almost never works in an Emerging environment.

In the Emerging organization there are always intact work groups that are eager to change, and they can set the example for the rest of the organization to follow.

Broad-based approach in Total Commitment organizations

Let us look at the example of our heart-attack victim one more time. As he is being discharged from the hospital, the doctor might give him some things to consider. She might say, "You survived the heart attack, but now there are some very specific areas you need to work on for a full recovery. You need to adopt a more healthy diet, exercise more frequently, and reduce your stress level. What you need to do is *change your lifestyle.*"

Total Commitment organizations can successfully embrace a change in lifestyle. They are able to make broad-based improvements because they have an aligned vision, management involvement, employee empowerment, customer focus, and a well-defined process—all the characteristics of empowered cultures.

Figure 3—Aligned Organizations

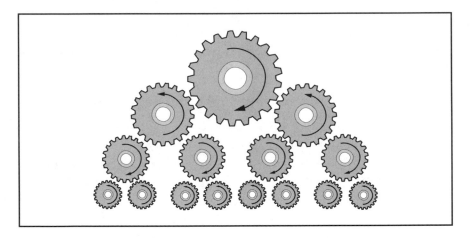

It is actually quite easy to visualize this as in **Figure 3** above. Picture a traditional hierarchical organization chart, with the president on top, the vice presidents next, and some directors after that. Imagine that the president's box is replaced by a large gear. Next, the vice presidents' boxes are replaced by smaller gears which are linked to the president's gear. Next, imagine successively smaller and smaller gears added and engaged as you go farther and farther down the chart.

If the largest gear at the top of the chart turns just a little, what do the smallest gears at the bottom of the chart do? They spin fast! That is because the gears are all configured—*and aligned*—properly. They all turn cooperatively, helping the organization to work effectively as a unit.

This enables the organization to attempt larger scale initiatives and actually achieve success. Unfortunately, there are very few organizations, particularly large ones, that are at this level of readiness. And, as we will see in **Chapter 10**, attempting this kind of broad-based approach before an organization is ready can lead to disastrous results.

Exercise—Improvement Activities

It is important to learn from the initiatives attempted in the past—whether or not they were successful. In fact, it is not uncommon to experience false starts. These give you the best opportunity to improve your approach to change—failure is almost always a much better teacher than success.

On **pages 44-46**, list at least three change initiatives that you have attempted in the past.

Chapter 10 addresses the issue of mismatching approach to readiness level and will show you how this can lead to disappointing results and even greater resistance.

Work Sheet 6—Improvement Activities

Case 1

Instructions: Describe a change or improvement initiative you have attempted and the results you achieved. Include the dates these efforts started and ended. Then for each one, write some general observations about how well the approach worked, how it was received by the organization, how it was positioned by the leadership, and any other pertinent comments.

Next list the tangible results that came from these programs and your opinion about whether or not the results were adequate.

Improvement initiative _____

_____

_____

General observations (How did it work, how was it received?)

_____

_____

Results (Describe successes and failures or benefits and shortcomings)

_____

_____

Were these results adequate? _____

_____

_____

What have I learned from this experience?_____

_____

_____

Case 2

Instructions: See case 1.

Improvement initiative _____

_____

_____

General observations (How did it work, how was it received?)

_____

_____

Results (Describe successes and failures or benefits and shortcomings)

_____

_____

Were these results adequate? _____

_____

_____

What have I learned from this experience?_____

_____

_____

Case 3

Instructions: See case 1.

Improvement initiative _____

_____

_____

General observations (How did it work, how was it received?)

_____

_____

Results (Describe successes and failures or benefits and shortcomings)

_____

_____

Were these results adequate? _____

_____

_____

What have I learned from this experience?_____

_____

_____

10

The Impact of Mismatching Approach and Readiness

There are many approaches to change that can be applied in any given situation. However, an approach that works successfully in one case may fail in another. Mismatching an organization's level of readiness to its approach to implementing change can set the organization back even more than if *nothing at all* had been done! Take a look at the following example.

Scenario

Imagine you are riding your bicycle through a scenic, hilly area. You start heading downhill. You are going really fast. You shift gears so that you have the large chain ring in front and the smallest cog on the freewheel on back. With this configuration, you are able to keep peddling even as the bike picks up speed.

As you approach the bottom of the hill, you are racing at top speed. The road starts going uphill. You do not change gears even though the terrain is changing. The road continues uphill, and you begin to lose speed. You still do not change gears. You try peddling harder, but the hill is too steep. You stand on the peddles, but that strategy does not work either. Finally, the bike loses all momentum and you fall to the ground.

Was the bicycle at fault? Of course not! As the terrain changed, you failed to change gears to match the hill before you. Just like this example, how many times have you heard someone complain about a change program that failed miserably because the method that was used by the organization was flawed?

Was the method really inadequate? Or was it just the wrong approach for the organization at that time. Just as the gear configuration was perfect for racing downhill, it was horribly inadequate for going uphill.

An approach that works exceptionally well in one situation can be a dismal failure in another. This is a very important lesson because many of the failures that companies experience when they try to implement change are because of a mismatch between the approach and the readiness level of the organization.

Look at **Figure 4** below. On the left side are the three levels of Organizational Maturity™—Firefighting, Emerging, and Total Commitment. Across the top are the three types of general approaches to change—Problem-solving, Focused change, and Broad-based change. The checkmarks indicate the recommended approach to change based on the level of the organization. The boxes marked with an "X" represent mismatches of approach and readiness as you will see in the following examples.

Figure 4—Level of Organization versus Approach

Readiness Level	Approach		
	Problem-solving	Focused change	Broad-based change
Firefighting	✓	✗	✗
Emerging	✗	✓	✗
Total Commitment	✗	✗	✓

We will now examine three organizations at the Firefighting, Emerging, and Total Commitment levels from the scenarios in **Chapter 8**. You will see what happens when we apply each of the following approaches—problem-solving, focused change, and broad-based change—to each type of organization.

Firefighting organization

Previously, we talked about a state agency, an example of a Firefighting group. The agency had a lot of direct contact between employees and its customer groups. Service was consistently poor, and the agency was getting a lot of vocal complaints from customers who were having various problems at a time when funding was a major issue in the state legislature. The situation had become critical.

Problem-solving

The approach to take with this organization is problem-solving. The agency needs to begin to measure the number and types of complaints it is getting from its customer groups. This will enable it to analyze the data to determine the critical issues.

Once the data is analyzed, the agency can then begin to make fundamental, short-term improvements to correct the processes that have allowed these problems to arise in the first place.

This is a basic problem-solving approach, and it is the best way to get things in order as a first step towards initiating more significant improvement activities. The organization can then begin to look at a more focused approach to deploying change initiatives.

Focused change

If this group took a broader approach and tried to address a major component of its operation, the results would be fairly predictable and would probably not meet the proposed objectives.

There might be a few people who would be interested—even excited—about working to improve their work methods, but most of them would be wary. Also, they would probably be just too busy to take on any additional responsibilities beyond their normal work load.

The people who were enthusiastic about the project could allocate time to improve processes associated with customer interaction, or they could even form customer focus groups. Unfortunately, they would probably run into resistance when they presented their recommendations to their management team. Ultimately, those who had embraced this project would become frustrated.

Broad-based change

This situation is like throwing a twenty-five ton pump into a sinking rowboat to help bail out the water. What happens when you do this? The boat sinks faster! The same thing happens when Firefighting organizations attempt to roll out broad-based change initiatives. They are sure to sink because the organization is not yet ready to deal with the enormity of the challenges created.

Take the example of the director of the state agency we talked about previously. He decides to attend a conference where he is exposed to a few different models for improvement. He sees one he really likes and decides to roll it out in his organization when he returns.

He calls his management team together and explains how this approach will transform the group. All employees will go through a three-day training program to become familiar with the model, and then the managers will form teams to address the major components of the model. Team members will spend about 20 percent of their time working on this effort. Of course, this will be in addition to their normal work load.

While the director has the right idea, he is really ignoring the organization's current reality. An approach like this would clearly be useless. Where you can, it is important to have management on board for improvement, but it is also important to consider what the organization is capable of supporting. If you try to do too much too soon, the efforts usually backfire and employees become cynical and less willing to support the next initiative—even if it is better-suited to the needs of the group.

Summary

Organizations that are in the Firefighting mode require a disciplined, structured approach to become stable. A problem-solving approach will give them the focus and information they need to succeed.

Emerging organization

In the example of the Emerging organization, a division of a large corporation had product quality problems, but compensated for them somewhat with excellent customer support.

This organization shows the defining characteristics of an Emerging organization. There is a clear split between groups that demonstrate what it takes to satisfy customers and stay in business and groups that do not.

Problem-solving

In an organization like this, there is a good chance that management has some experience with the problem-solving approach, at least in the groups that are showing progress. Focusing on this as a catalyst could help the groups that are struggling. However, this approach could penalize the groups ready for something a little more aggressive by limiting them to basic techniques in change and improvement.

At this point in the group's evolution, the basic problem-solving approach should be used as a part of the change initiatives, as one of the many tools at its disposal.

Focused change

A focused change approach will produce the best results in this type of organization. Let us look at the situation again.

In the above organization, the customer response group has been recognized by its customers for providing outstanding service, even though there have been some concerns regarding product quality. This team can make a greater contribution to the division because it already has demonstrated progress towards improvement.

In an organization such as this, you can start your effort by meeting with management and staff members of that team. Because they appear to have a handle on their own area, it is very likely that they have already recognized the weak interface points in other areas of the division.

Tell the members that because of their recognized leadership, you would like to work with them to make their contribution to the division even more significant and more widely recognized. Since they probably have many of the components of a comprehensive management system already in place, you might recommend a self-assessment. This approach would validate their strengths and identify, in an objective manner, areas they need to address for improvement.

When you have identified specific actions, work with the team members to develop specific training, implementation, and follow-up plans. Establish metrics that will measure progress on implementing the program and on the actual business impact. Finally, get them to begin thinking about how they will communicate their initiative and ultimately their results to the rest of the organization to serve as a model for others to follow.

A group that has been successful in the absence of a formal change program already has the mind-set to succeed with this approach. Placing its efforts in a broader context will energize it to do even more to improve the effectiveness of the group and lead the rest of the organization.

Broad-based change

There are some groups in an Emerging organization that might benefit from a broadly deployed approach to change and might even have the bandwidth to make it work. However, there will be at least as many groups that will be so buried in Firefighting activities that they would be dragged down by the effort.

Deploying an organization-wide broad-based initiative is very complicated and requires that virtually all parts of the organization be at a high level of readiness. Because of the level of interdependence required for these kinds of initiatives to succeed, a lack of interest, enthusiasm, and participation from even a few groups will almost certainly lead to failure.

Summary

Emerging organizations are like adolescents—somewhere between childhood and adulthood. Parts of them are mature enough to begin taking on broader responsibilities, but other parts are still clinging to less mature ways of operating.

By identifying the groups that are ready to change and helping them to succeed, these organizations can continue to mature and take on broader initiatives. A focused change approach enables improvement to take place and sets the example for other parts of the organization to emulate.

Total Commitment organization

Our Total Commitment example involved a small local college and its high-level plans for the future. It was ready for an orchestrated, broad-based approach to change that would see involvement from all levels and all parts of the organization.

Problem-solving

Focusing on simple analytical techniques like statistical analysis or approaches based on correcting individual problems would really hold this group back from what it is capable of accomplishing.

While certainly no harm will come from focusing on these types of techniques, the return on the investment of time and effort could be disappointing. In all likelihood, these groups have already passed through a phase in their development where they had to work through tough issues using these simple approaches. They have proved that they are able to sustain the performance needed to take them to the next level.

Focused change

What typically happens in a focused change approach is that individual groups select issues that they feel will best enhance the performance and effectiveness of their own group. They may consider how their actions can help other teams, but the focus is generally directed to their particular group during the initial phases of deployment.

The danger of deploying a focused change approach in a Total Commitment organization is that almost all of the component groups are at a high level of readiness. If all of these groups individually select areas to address, there is the very real possibility that some of them may be redundant, leading to a duplication of effort; some of them may be conflicting; and some of them may even cancel each other out without anyone really being aware that this is happening.

Broad-based change

When an entire organization is aligned around a clearly defined set of objectives and is given the tools to succeed, the results can be amazing. Harnessing and coordinating the efforts of a diverse set of groups is the key to large-scale success.

The approach of a top-down deployment, though, can succeed only in the Total Commitment organization. The alignment of the organization must permit it to be flexible and responsive to a changing environment. Maintaining clear focus on the vision and staying aware of the changing environment will enhance the probability for long-term success.

Summary

In a Total Commitment company, it is imperative to maintain the momentum. There are many factors that continually threaten the ability of an organization to operate at the Total Commitment level. While the actual cases of Total Commitment companies are rare, in those cases where broad-based change strategies are utilized, these companies are able to harness the capabilities of the entire organization.

Part 4

How to Overcome
Roadblocks

11

Understanding the Challenges

Why is change so difficult?

In high school, a fellow student was taking an advanced placement calculus course and was having trouble handling the extra work involved. When he expressed his concerns to the teacher, she said, "That's why this is an advanced placement course—if it was easy, anyone could do it!"

While this may sound extreme, and even somewhat elitist, it also happens to be true. And the same thing can be said of bringing about successful change— if it was easy, anyone could do it.

Change is difficult. Period. Change in an organizational setting requires people to change their attitudes, work processes, habits, and interactions with their coworkers, customers, and suppliers. Frequently, it also requires the ability to change *other* people's behavior and this can be challenging.

In discussions with people about change, a litany of reasons, justifications, and excuses are put forth as to why it will not work, as described in **Chapter 3** on roadblocks.

We have presented the basics on how to select the most appropriate approach to change for your group. Now it is time to revisit these roadblocks and offer recommendations on how to address them.

Some roadblocks stand by themselves, while others share common elements. Those which share common elements have been grouped together in separate chapters. You can readily see the common approaches they use. Often, if an organization has one symptom, it probably has one or more of the others.

Take a few minutes now to identify the roadblocks that are impeding your progress in deploying change and learn how you can overcome them.

12

**Supporting a Group That
Reports to Someone Else**

How can you help a group promote change?

One of the most difficult jobs you can have is to be responsible for the change initiatives of a group that does not report directly to you. You may work for the quality or human resources department and have the best interests of the group at heart when you offer your assistance. Yet, when you approach the group with a cheerful, "Hi! I'm from Quality; I'm here to help!" the members of the group quickly disappear because their experience tells them that this kind of *help* just means more work.

To be successful in this role, it is essential to first understand the group's overall level of readiness and to use this information as an indication of exactly how you *can* help. More importantly, you need to know how your assistance will be perceived by the group you are supporting.

Many of the other roadblocks that will be discussed in the following chapters are endemic to only one or two of the readiness levels. This situation—where you support a group that reports to someone else—can occur in organizations at all three levels. Because of this, we will provide specific strategies for all three levels.

Refer to **Figure 5** on **page 60** to see how different levels require different approaches and have different points of influence.

Firefighting

In the Firefighting organization, the problems are urgent and abundant. As you have already learned, anything that is introduced will add to the already overwhelming work load and will cause concern and resistance.

Your best approach in this situation is to select the groups in the most serious trouble and ask yourself—and the group—what you can do to help to address its current problems. This will accomplish two critical things for both you and the group.

First, it will become a collaborative effort to help the group work its way through a very difficult situation. Whatever it is that caused the problems, you will have worked together as a team to help solve it and get closer to stable ground.

Figure 5—Strategies for Success

Phase	Recommended Approaches	Target Groups	Benefits to Organization	Measurement Recommendations
Firefighting	Problem-solving	Problem groups	Solve their current problems	Number of problems Number of solutions Employee satisfaction Customer responsiveness
Emerging	Focused change	Recognized innovators	Lead the organization	Baseline measurements Performance targets Quality metrics
Total Commitment	Broad-based change	Senior management	Transform the organization	Self-assessment results Financial results Customer satisfaction Employee satisfaction

Second, collaborating to solve problems will help establish you as a valuable, contributing member of the team, not an outsider trying to make the group members' lives more difficult. When the group stabilizes enough to begin to invest in focused change initiatives, it will accept and most likely seek your input on what to do next and how to best approach it. After all, you are now a member of the team.

Emerging

You will recall that the unique distinguishing characteristic of the Emerging organization is that there are intact work groups that are ready, able, and willing to begin making tangible changes in their approach to work.

If you are trying to facilitate an organization at this level of readiness, target the groups that seem to be ready—the early innovators—and work with them. They will be more willing to take the first steps; they will benefit from the tangible results; and they will appreciate the visibility these results will bring to the group.

Encourage these groups to establish measurements to evaluate the success of the initiative and to show results, not just effort. When the time comes to demonstrate the effectiveness of the group's approach, nothing will be more convincing than tangible, measurable business results.

As you continue to be a part of their success, you will be in a position to help steer them in the right direction towards further improvement.

Total Commitment

An organization that has all its gears properly engaged is able to take steps on a larger scale. In this case, you can work with the organization's senior managers to help coordinate broad-based initiatives that can only be effective in the Total Commitment organization.

In this case, your role will be to plan and coordinate the program with the general support of the organization's senior management. Your goal will be to help make major breakthroughs and take the organization in new directions that will have a significant impact on future success.

13

Empowering Change
Without Management Support

Is management support necessary?

A comment I hear frequently from groups is, "This all sounds reasonable, but don't we need senior management support to really make this work?" It is as if these groups are waiting for the *empowerment fairy* to fly by, wave her magic wand, and then things will happen automatically.

While you do need a certain level of support from management to proceed, the level of support required is not nearly as significant as you might think. Even with minimal or nonexistent support, change can happen.

Roadblock: Without support there can be no change
Approach: Empower yourself!

It is possible to virtually empower yourself to make change happen. In fact, most people have potentially more freedom and authority than they

Figure 6—Organization Chart

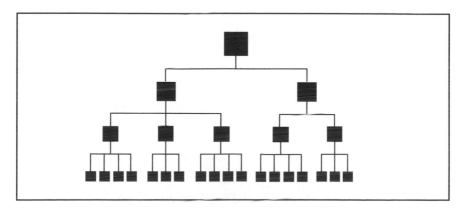

think they do to accomplish their work objectives. This same idea applies to individuals and groups attempting change. For example, look at the organization chart in **Figure 6** on the previous page. Assume that the top person in the organization is unable or unwilling to support the change initiative. Does this mean that nothing can happen? No, what it does mean is that the organization is almost certainly not at the Total Commitment level of readiness.

But should you give up? Absolutely not! Drop down one level in the chart. Is that person or organization ready? Sooner or later you will get to a point where the readiness level is sufficiently high to enable the necessary changes to take place.

The circled area of the chart represents the organization ready for change as shown in **Figure 7**. To the extent possible, imagine that the circled portion of the organization is a stand-alone group. Recognize that you are still part of the whole company and that you still depend on its infrastructure and support services. This is not an excuse to return to an old-style, silo-based structure, but rather an invitation to view your group as an empowered independent entity.

Figure 7—Subgroup of Organization Chart

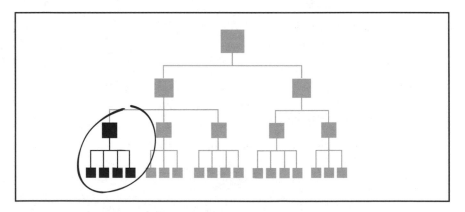

Now, look again at the top of the subgroup. What is the new role of the senior most person? President! Now you have the leadership support you need to move forward successfully!

It is all a matter of perspective. In any organization, regardless of the level of readiness, there is always at least one innovative group that can begin to evolve its processes and methods to make a tangible impact on the rest of the organization and act as a springboard for other groups.

14

Addressing the Organizational Culture

How do you keep up with current trends in organizations?

New approaches common to many businesses over the last several years include: a shift from functional orientation to process orientation, from individual reward and recognition to team reward and recognition, from rewards based on short-term performance to rewards based on long-term results, and from rewarding blind effort to rewarding results.

These changes have evolved naturally in some organizations in response to competitive pressures or changes in the business landscape. In other organizations, they have not yet begun. Although the latter situation makes it difficult to initiate change and see it through, change is still possible.

Roadblock: Function versus process organization
Approach: Involve other groups

When the organization is modeled on an old-style *silo* mentality, where the group functions in a virtual vacuum without any interaction with other groups, the Organizational Maturity™ model can still be effective. You must use the approach described in **Chapter 13** where you focus on the function or functions over which you have some direct influence.

As you focus your efforts on improvements in your group, try to involve representatives from other groups that are upstream and downstream from you in the overall process.

Even though these other groups may be difficult to work with, you will probably have one or two allies who will work with you to develop solutions that will benefit the organization as a whole.

The key is to make sure the solutions will help these other groups as well as your own so everyone benefits from the effort.

Roadblock: Rewards based on individual versus team performance
Approach: Focus on team recognition

One common roadblock to change is that the organization rewards individuals often at the expense of team accomplishments—or team burnout. Once again, try to set the example from within your own group, and let others follow your lead.

A former colleague of mine developed a novel approach to applying the organization's employee evaluation process in his group. Instead of using it to set individual goals and measure individual performance, he used it to establish *team* goals and measure *team* performance.

He still followed the guidelines and timetables established for the process, but he simply shifted the focus from the individual to the team. While somewhat frightening at first—for both his managers and his staff—there were some tangible benefits. Most notably, the team members started supporting each other. When one person was having problems completing his assignment, other members of the team would rally to help, instead of complaining to the manager.

And, by the way, the team met its objectives for the year. If you preach the importance of teamwork, try to reflect this philosophy in your reward and recognition programs as well.

Roadblock: Rewards based on short-term performance
Approach: Match compensation to long-term results

This can be a very difficult situation to overcome because most improvement and change initiatives—at least the meaningful ones—do not produce quick, immediate results. There is no one magic solution. Unfortunately, a constant focus on short-term results will make it difficult, if not impossible, to get the support you need to begin to change.

Many organizations' compensation systems are based on relatively short-term measurements. End-of-year evaluations for performance ratings, salary increases, and possible bonuses are based on the degree to which employees complete their objectives for that year.

While this is an appropriate goal for individual contributors at lower levels of the organization, it seems somewhat inadequate for managers with greater scope and authority.

If you have someone with the title of *director* you might assume that the person's responsibility is to provide long-term direction—hence the title. If, however, you reward a person who has long-term responsibility based upon short-term results, it is fairly predictable which areas will hold that leader's attention. Linking a manager's compensation to performance over an appropriate time frame helps ensure the proper focus.

Roadblock: Rewarding effort instead of results
Approach: Be clear on what is being recognized

In some organizations, managers may recognize an employee's efforts with *spot awards*, which may include a cash bonus or a gift certificate. These awards are sometimes challenged by other employees who feel that the behavior the managers are rewarding as exceptional is actually the person's regular job.

Managers may also recognize employees who have worked nights and weekends to *put out fires* only to find that it is these same individuals who have caused the problems in the first place.

As organizations become more and more sensitive to this issue, they will more closely examine exactly what constitutes a successful change initiative or tangible improvement in the operation. Then they can begin to reward employees for impacting results and not just the effort put forth.

To position your efforts as something worthwhile and effective, ensure that you have clear, objective measurements to support your efforts. You will not get any credit for the time and money you have spent if you cannot demonstrate a clear return on the investment.

15

Managing the
Change Blockers

How do you overcome resistance to change?

At any stage in an organization's trek along the maturity curve, you will encounter people—frequently from within the management ranks—who will resist any attempt to change. This can occur for two major reasons: *caught in the middle* and *underminers*.

Roadblock: Caught in the middle
Approach: Make the right thing to do be the easy thing to do

In many cases, managers in the middle levels of the organization structure find themselves sandwiched between their commitment to improve the organization and pressure from above to make deliverable dates.

The people below them on the organization chart know that things have to change because they face the fallout of the current system on a daily basis—stress, burnout, ten- to twelve-hour days, and seventy-hour weeks. The people at the higher levels know things need to change because they are accountable to a board of directors, the financial community, or a legislative oversight committee.

In the middle, however, there is a dilemma. It comes down to the fact that people have faith in what has worked for them in the past and, in general, will not change without a very good reason.

It is similar to the situation that occurs in cartoons when the character is faced with a difficult choice. Help usually appears on the character's shoulders in the form of an angel and a devil.

The same thing happens to middle level managers. The angel whispers, "You have to change! You have to improve! If you don't, the organization will lose momentum and come to a grinding halt!"

As the manager begins to nod his head in agreement, the devil shouts, "Don't be an idiot! There's no reason to change—just continue to do things the way you've always done them—after all, that's how you got to be a vice-president in the first place!"

What worked before may have been an adequate response to the situation as it existed at that time. If the situation is different today—and it almost certainly is—the same response will deliver results that will be at best disappointing and, at worst, disastrous.

If you find yourself facing this roadblock, follow the advice from one of my previous managers: make the *right* thing to do be the *easy* thing to do. If you need cooperation from these change blockers, find a way to make the outcome benefit *them*. Many people have a *what's in it for me* attitude. Although unfortunate, you can use it to your advantage. If your change initiative is consistent with the mission and values of the organization, everyone will benefit, and the change blocker may even become an ally.

Roadblock: Underminers—dinosaurs, relics, and artifacts
Approach: Set them free or let them be

The second kind of change blocker you may encounter will frequently surface as the organization makes its way out of the Emerging phase and into the Total Commitment phase. At this point in the organization's evolution, people who have not made the commitment to change will identify themselves loudly and clearly.

They will take any opportunity to undermine the initiative in public and in private, they will sabotage the work that has been done, and they will come up with every imaginable justification for their behavior—ostensibly in the best interests of the organization.

These people have nice names for themselves: traditional managers and classical managers. But they are really dinosaurs, relics, and artifacts. And there is only one thing to do: set them free. While this might sound extreme, it is in the best interests of the organization to let them go. They generally hold the company back because they do not support the improvement initiatives that could move the company forward.

If you do not have the authority to set them free, then try an approach that will benefit their best interests. If that does not work, remember that it is sometimes easier to get forgiveness than permission. Move forward and deal with the fallout. If the outcome is all that you anticipated, then your results will speak for themselves.

16

Overcoming Head in the Sand Management

How do you make change happen without resources?

The roadblocks described in this chapter are all indicative of a management structure that wants results but is not willing to provide financial support. Sometimes, this unwillingness to support change may result from the realities of the environment in which the organization is currently operating. Other times, it may only be a case of an unenlightened management team. Nearly always, these examples occur in Firefighting situations.

There are several approaches to address these issues.

Roadblock: The "do more with less" approach
Approach: Take small steps

In the case where the organization has cut positions, delayed hiring, or taken on additional work without adequate staffing, the organization is pressured to do more with less. Interestingly enough, management will insist that this is not the case, and the objective here, actually, is to *work smarter not harder.*

In this situation, move very slowly and take small steps towards implementing change. Use the Firefighting approach of attacking the areas that will have an immediate effect on the organization. As you become more successful and the organization matures, you will be able to take on even broader issues. Until then, larger-scale programs simply will not survive.

Roadblock: No training—just get better!
Approach: Find other ways to provide training

In this situation, the group is instructed to do better and to work smarter, even though it has no idea how to accomplish this. This is similar to the response you give to your child about his poor report card; he had better improve his grades by the next reporting period—or else. If you do not take the time to understand what is causing the bad grades, and if you do not take any action to address the root causes, how can you expect the report card to be different next time?

There may be valid reasons for a lack of training in an organization. If funding is limited, then work with what the situation allows. Unfortunately, this is a time when additional training is really necessary, and you may not be in a position to make this decision.

In this case the best approach is to identify the specific skills that are needed and use existing resources to provide them to the team. There are many ways of providing training that do not involve spending money. In-house computer-based training, a buddy system, and lunchtime learning sessions provided by knowledgeable members of the group can all fill the gap and can help provide the skills necessary to promote change.

Roadblock: Too busy
Approach: Wait until the right time or make it the right time

Sometimes, there is just so much going on that it is simply not possible to take on another work initiative. If there is too much work to be accomplished to allow any time to invest in a change initiative, then wait until time frees up. For instance, an accounting firm may not want to start any change initiatives during tax season. When the work load eases, there may be more time available to dedicate to an improvement initiative.

Unfortunately, if the work load is static and unchanging, then this kind of high demand environment will continue. If this is your situation, set priorities and, if possible, begin by taking small steps that will take a minimal amount of time. As the changes begin to have an impact, there may be more free time available because less time is being spent fighting fires. As you progress from a Firefighting to an Emerging organization, you will be able to broaden the scope of your change initiatives.

Roadblock: There is not enough money in the budget
Approach: Start small and do what you can

It is a fact of life that business considerations can hinder improvement and change initiatives. While it is true that *quality is free* from a long-term return on investment perspective, doing *anything* in an organization requires an investment of time and money of some kind.

The irony of this is that organizations that are in tough financial straits are the ones that most need to take some action now. If there are truly no resources to be found, then start small and target areas that can be addressed with minimal outlay.

Apply the Firefighting strategy of problem-solving to address the areas most in need of attention. It may be necessary to ask people to invest additional time to accomplish this. In a situation where they are probably already putting in extra hours, you must make absolutely certain that the efforts you are suggesting will have clear and immediate impact in addressing the problem areas.

Roadblock: Change as an event—not a process
Approach: Disguise a large initiative as a series of smaller ones

Many organizations view change activities as discrete events rather than ongoing processes. Our culture has a quick-fix mentality—we like to find the one solution that will address all of our problems. This is true in our personal lives, as well as in our professional lives.

This concept manifests itself in the workplace as an intense focus on a particular initiative followed by a huge sigh of relief when it is finally completed. Unfortunately, this view of change is naive—change by its very nature is dynamic and is a journey more than a destination.

If you find yourself operating in an organization with this kind of mentality, recognize that you can cleverly disguise a long-term, continuous process as a series of linked, interrelated discrete *mini-processes*, each with its own distinct and recognizable ending point.

You can engineer the deployment of your initiative to reflect the particular readiness level of the groups you are working with, targeting each piece to the needs of each group while still making progress towards a comprehensive long-term strategy.

With this approach, you can realize the long-term benefits of a broad-based approach while working within the constraints of your situation.

Roadblock: Success
Approach: Find the innovators

One of the most difficult situations is a successful organization that sees no reason to change. There are two distinct examples of this: one where the organization has achieved this success as the result of a carefully planned and executed long-range plan, and one where success just fell into its lap.

In the first case, where there was a strategic plan for success, there may actually be no real need for dramatic change. There are organizations that have clearly defined processes that drive their organizations to outstanding and sustainable results. In these situations, only minor adjustments may be necessary until the organizations are ready to branch out in new directions. At that point, the Total Commitment approach will be appropriate.

In the second case, the rapid growth and unprecedented success that the organization realized may only be a short-lived bit of serendipity. If your success is a result of being in the right place at the right time, and you do not have a sustainable model to follow, then eventually it will be the wrong place or the wrong time. Just as rapidly as you ascended to the top of the heap, you may find your organization sputtering toward the bottom.

In these groups it is best to identify the forward-thinking leaders who will not be content with the status quo—as good as it may be. These leaders will likely recognize that the success of the organization is a result of good fortune and will be looking for a way to solidify this success and make it sustainable over the long term.

17

Combating the Flavor of the Month Initiative

How do you gain commitment with conflicting approaches?

A classic problem that many large organizations face at some time, and often repeatedly, is the introduction of one initiative after another without a clear direction of where the organization is headed. Once the featured initiative of the month/quarter/year has achieved its initial results, it is discarded, and soon a new one takes its place. Employees are skeptical of any new program because they know it will soon be replaced by yet another new initiative.

Roadblock: Flavor of the month approach with competing initiatives
Approach: Plan carefully—after a suitable mourning period

Introducing one initiative after another creates the perception that there is no real long-term commitment to a single approach. It promotes an attitude that encourages people to pay lip service to the current initiative, commit the minimal effort needed to be perceived as a team player, or ignore the initiative altogether, knowing that it will be replaced soon by another one, and another one after that.

Sometimes, the new program begins even before the first one is completed. There may be multiple initiatives in play concurrently, as they compete for attention and resources and provide conflicting objectives.

There are two things you need to do. First, recognize that the problem exists; second, plan *very carefully* before you introduce anything else. Make certain that the approach taken is appropriate for the group's level of readiness and be clear on the objectives and expectations of the initiative.

It may be much more effective in the long run to actually *delay* introduction of a new approach until the group has had time to recover from the previous attempt at change. If you do not, then when the next sincere effort comes along, people will not see the promise and benefits possible. They will only remember with disdain the time and money thrown away on the last effort.

Roadblock: Premature training
Approach: Plan ahead for just-in-time learning

Premature training is one of the nasty side effects of taking on a change initiative for which the group is not yet ready. In fact, this is the most visible one and the one that in retrospect will be remembered as a major *waste of time*.

If you put an entire organization through three days of training on a new program that the organization cannot sustain, not only do you waste three days of people's time, but you also waste the *opportunity cost* of the work they did not accomplish while they were in training.

Use the Organizational Maturity™ model to identify the most appropriate approach to change. You will be able to provide the necessary training in a just-in-time manner to give your employees the skills and knowledge they need to be successful at a time when they are best able to use them.

Roadblock: Fear of working oneself out of a job
Approach: Don't worry!

One common concern presented as an argument for keeping the status quo is that if groups become too efficient, they could actually improve themselves out of their jobs because efficiencies in the process could render their roles redundant.

This issue is probably emotional residue remaining from the many organizations that used reengineering as a euphemism for downsizing. In these cases, it was not any efficiencies that eliminated their positions; rather it was the organization's need to address short-term financial concerns.

The recommendation is, "Don't worry!" The fact is, if you are capable of successfully initiating change and dealing proactively instead of reactively with a dynamic business environment, you possess the skill set that is actively sought by most enlightened businesses today.

18

Tailoring the Approach
to the Organization

How do you approach change for your unique situation?

To people who respond to change efforts by saying, "It will never work here—our organization is different," or "Organizations have different issues," I usually shout, "Exactly!" This usually startles them but it also stuns them enough so they can absorb the key point of this model: all organizations are different, and what works in one organization under one set of circumstances will almost certainly *not* work in another organization with another set of challenges.

Roadblock: It will never work here—our organization is different
Approach: Tailor the approach to the needs of the group

Your organization is very different from any other organization; and because of that, your strategy for initiating change will be unique to your organization. That is why it is important to select a program that meets the specific needs of the particular group, not because another company had great success with it. Your level of readiness is probably different from the other company's and, therefore, your approach should be different as well. In fact, as you already know, this issue is at the heart of the entire Organizational Maturity™ model!

To overcome this roadblock, tell management that it is probably right; that the specific approach it might be considering may not work for your group at your level of readiness.

In the following chapters, you will identify the level of readiness of your group and of the organization to which your group reports. Then you will determine the approach that works best for you. The action-planning section will help you select a relevant and meaningful area to address.

Part 5

Where Are You Now?

- Chapter 19—Assessing Your Level of Organizational Maturity™

- Chapter 20—Selecting the Best Scope for Your Group

- Chapter 21—Group versus Company Readiness

19

Assessing Your Level of Organizational Maturity™

Identify your group and company readiness levels

Now that you understand the basic model of Organizational Maturity™ and recognize the potential roadblocks you may face, you can start to use it to identify the most appropriate approach to use to initiate real change.

Exercise—Self-assessment tool

Work Sheet 7 on **page 83** is a tool to assess Organizational Maturity™. It has two statements for each of the five characteristics of empowered cultures: vision alignment, management involvement, employee empowerment, customer focus, and process base.

Rate your individual group, as well as your whole company, for each of these statements using a scale from 1 to 5, with 5 being high.

For example, if, as you read the statement you think, "Yeah, right, we might do that in 25 years..." then you should give it a low score of 1 or 2. If, on the other hand, you think, "This really sounds like us..." then you would give it a higher score of 3, 4, or 5.

To understand how Organizational Maturity™ influences your approach to change, it is important to identify your own group's readiness level, as well as that of the larger organization of which your group is a part.

To determine the definition for group that applies best in your situation, start by identifying that part of the organization over which you have direct influence. This may be your work group, department, or division. If you are an individual contributor, the scope of your direct influence may be limited to your own job or function.

"Group," in this context, refers to whatever part of the organization you can personally and directly influence.

Identifying the context for "company" is fairly straightforward: it is simply the next higher organizational unit. That is, it is the function to which the "group" reports.

For example, you may be the general manager of a subsidiary. In this case, the subsidiary would be the "group" and the corporate parent would be the "company." If you are the division director of a state agency, the division is the "group" and the organization to which your division reports would be the "company." To refresh your memory, you may want to refer back to **Work Sheet 1** on **page 6** and review your definitions from before.

As discussed earlier, it is important to understand the readiness level of a group to know how best to facilitate change. But when you also consider the relationship between group and company readiness, the course of action becomes very clear.

Work Sheet 7—Organizational Maturity™ Assessment

Instructions: Score each of the ten statements on **page 83** for your group and your company on a scale from 1 to 5 with 5 being high. Total the scores and then put a checkmark in the box that corresponds to the level of Organizational Maturity™ indicated by your score for both your group and your company. If you scored between 10 and 23, the level would be Firefighting. Emerging ranges from 24 to 37 and Total Commitment would be 38 to 50. This information will be used in **Part 6**.

Group level of readiness

❏ Firefighting 10-23   ❏ Emerging 24-37   ❏ Total Commitment 38-50

Company level of readiness

❏ Firefighting 10-23   ❏ Emerging 24-37   ❏ Total Commitment 38-50

Work Sheet 7—Organizational Maturity™ Assessment

Characteristics of High-performance Organizations	Group	Company
Vision Alignment 1. The organization has a clear statement of its vision, mission, and values which has been communicated to and is understood and accepted by all employees.		
2. All employees understand the link between their job functions and the organization's vision.		
Management Involvement 3. The organization's senior management is committed to the vision and has articulated its short- and long-term objectives in related areas.		
4. Management demonstrates its personal commitment through active and visible involvement in change activities and through the focus placed on these activities in team meetings.		
Employee Empowerment 5. Employees feel empowered to identify, communicate, and implement actions that improve the overall effectiveness of the organization.		
6. Management believes that all employees have valuable input to contribute in determining the success of the organization and recognizes employee contributions.		
Customer Focus 7. Employees are familiar with major internal and external customer groups in both their group and the organization as a whole.		
8. Employees clearly understand how their jobs contribute to the overall satisfaction and effectiveness of all customer groups.		
Process Base 9. The processes used in performing individual work functions are well-documented and accurately reflect the work as it is actually being done.		
10. There is a formal mechanism for evaluating process adherence and effectiveness and for initiating improvements and corrective actions where necessary.		
Totals		

20

Selecting the Best Scope for Your Group

Evaluate your current situation and past failures

The first step to achieve any significant change is to begin with a clear understanding of your current situation. What are the challenges that are facing the group? Consider all areas including competitive, technical, economic, environmental, and societal. What is it that you are hoping to accomplish with the initiative? What will the environment look like if your initiative is successful?

Have a clear idea of what you are trying to accomplish in the group. Understanding your reasons for implementing change is an essential ingredient for success.

The next step in the process is to evaluate and understand what worked and, more importantly, what *did not* work with previous attempts at change. Many times, in retrospect, it was simply a matter of mismatching the approach and readiness.

Take a few minutes now to review **Work Sheet 2** on **page 8** and **Work Sheet 6** on **pages 44-46** to help you determine what worked and what did not work in the past when attempting change in your organization. This will help you understand where you are starting from on your journey.

Exercise—Select the best approach for your group

Now comes the time to select the type of approach you will use in deploying your change initiative in the "group." The readiness level of the "company" will be taken into account in **Chapter 21**.

Using the results from the Organizational Maturity™ Assessment, **Work Sheet 7** on **page 83**, complete **Work Sheet 8** on **page 86** to identify the general approach that will work best for your group.

Work Sheet 8—Selecting the Best Approach

Instructions: Answer the questions below to determine the best approach for your group.

1. From the exercise on **Work Sheet 7**, **page 83**, what was the result of Organizational Maturity™ assessment of your *group's* level of readiness?

   ❑ Firefighting   ❑ Emerging   ❑ Total Commitment

2. Based on your group's level of readiness, look at the table below and select the basic needs of your group.

   ❑ Survival   ❑ Healing   ❑ Change of Lifestyle

3. Based on your group's level of readiness, look at the table below and select the basic goal for your group.

   ❑ Stability   ❑ Mobilization   ❑ World Class Performance

4. Based on your group's level of readiness, look at the table below and select the type of approach recommended for your group?

   ❑ Problem-solving   ❑ Focused change   ❑ Broad-based change

Readiness Levels	Needs	Goals	Approach
Firefighting	Survival	Stability	Problem-solving
Emerging	Healing	Mobilization	Focused Change
Total Commitment	Change of Lifestyle	World Class Performance	Broad-based Change

21

Group versus Company Readiness

One of the fundamental concepts of this book is that all organizations are not at the same level of readiness for change. The obvious corollary is that within a given organization, different groups are at different levels of readiness and therefore need their own unique approach to change.

We have already used the model of Organizational Maturity™ to help you understand the basic approach you should use to implement your group's change initiatives, and you have gained an appreciation that, to a large extent, you can empower yourself to take positive action.

It is certainly critical to understand what general approach you should take for your group; but if you base your strategy solely on this information, you will have completely ignored the larger environment in which you are trying to make the change occur.

So how do you take into account both the readiness level of the individual group and the readiness level of the organization or company?

It is all about relationships

In developing the model of Organizational Maturity™, I had reached the point that we are now at: three levels of readiness with different needs and approaches for organizations at each level.

While it made sense that the level of readiness of a group would dictate a general approach to change, there was still the issue of what was going on in the rest of the organization.

For example, if the group was at a high readiness level, but the rest of the organization was in a Firefighting mode, it seemed unlikely that the individual group would be *allowed* to make significant changes. You can just imagine the conversation taking place.

You: Boss, we've just done an assessment of our group,
            found that we're at the Total Commitment level, and
            we're ready to begin a major program of enhancing
            our key business processes!
Boss: You have that much time on your hands? I have plenty
            of issues that need immediate attention! When you've
            finished with them, you can go ahead and try your
            "little change program."

A model was needed to explain *mismatches* in readiness levels. I drew
a chart with "company" across the top and "group" down the side, and I sat
and stared at the sheet trying to figure out what to put in the blanks.

Then it hit me. The model is like a relationship...a romantic relationship! Firefighting is like dating. While you are not serious about a long-
term commitment to change, you will flirt with the idea of making some
nominal improvements in the organization.

Emerging is like engagement. You are more serious about your improvement efforts, but you have not made a final commitment yet.

Total Commitment is like marriage. You are now ready to make a total
commitment to change. This model is illustrated in **Figure 8** below.

The shaded boxes indicate where both parties are at the same level of
understanding in their relationship. At the dating phase, the couple accepts

Figure 8—Group versus Company Readiness

Group Level (Person 1)	Company Level (Person 2)		
	Firefighting (Dating)	Emerging (Engagement)	Total Commitment (Marriage)
Firefighting (Dating)			
Emerging (Engagement)	**(B)**	**(A)**	
Total Commitment (Marriage)	▼		▲

that the relationship is a casual one with no real commitment. As the relationship matures, they progress into the engagement phase and then finally into marriage—a long-term, committed relationship. This evolution is represented by the line "A."

Problems arise when the individuals in the relationship are not at the same level of commitment. Suppose you have two people in a relationship. Both of them want to keep it casual. Usually this relationship works well because both have the same expectations. But what happens if, over time, one of the couple wants a longer-term commitment to the relationship, and the other person just wants to keep things casual? This mismatch is represented by line "B."

When one person wants a serious, committed relationship and the other wants a loose, casual one, normally the person who desires the commitment gets tired of the situation and ends the relationship. This is a classic case of a mismatched relationship.

Similar situations can occur, for example, in the case of a Total Commitment group in a Firefighting organization. The people who are ready for change will become fed up with their management's unwillingness to change and will either give up trying (apathy), do *exactly* what the boss wants (malicious compliance), or leave the organization.

It is much easier to select the right approach to change in organizations where the group and the company are at the same level of readiness. But you can initiate effective change even if they are not. Each of the nine situations in **Figure 9** has its own unique considerations and recommended course of action.

Figure 9—Group/Company Strategies

Group Level	Company Level		
	Firefighting	Emerging	Total Commitment
Firefighting	Sink or Swim	Catching Up	Desperate Measures
Emerging	Blazing the Trail	Forging Ahead	Follow the Leader
Total Commitment	Against the Wall	Pulling Through	Breaking Out

Exercise—Approach to Change

To find out your approach to change based on the readiness level of both your group and company, go to **Work Sheet 7, page 83**, and make a note of your levels for both group and company readiness. Then check the appropriate boxes in **Work Sheet 9** below. See where your readiness levels intersect. This will provide you with the recommended approach based on your group and company readiness levels.

Work Sheet 9—Choosing Your Approach to Change

Instructions: Check the level for both the group and company, circle the approach for change in the table, and write the approach in the statement below it.

1. What was your *group's* overall level of readiness?

   ❑ Firefighting   ❑ Emerging   ❑ Total Commitment

2. What was your *company's* overall level of readiness?

   ❑ Firefighting   ❑ Emerging   ❑ Total Commitment

	Company Level		
Group Level	**Firefighting**	**Emerging**	**Total Commitment**
Firefighting	Sink or Swim	Catching Up	Desperate Measures
Emerging	Blazing the Trail	Forging Ahead	Follow the Leader
Total Commitment	Against the Wall	Pulling Through	Breaking Out

3. My situation is best described as _____ .

Implementing the right approach

In the following chapters, each of the nine situations, from "Sink or Swim" to "Breaking Out," will be examined in order to provide you with a detailed approach on how to implement change within your organization. It will be explained using the following general format:

- Description of the situation
- An example
- The recommended approach
- How to position the effort with the group
- How to position the effort with management

This format will enable you to identify the exact situation in which you find yourself and will enable you to select the approach with the greatest likelihood for success.

For easy reference, the nine possible combinations and their subsequent chapters are summarized below.

Figure 10—The Right Approach

Situation	Group Readiness	Company Readiness	Chapter
Sink or Swim	Firefighting	Firefighting	22
Catching Up	Firefighting	Emerging	23
Desperate Measures	Firefighting	Total Commitment	24
Blazing the Trail	Emerging	Firefighting	25
Forging Ahead	Emerging	Emerging	26
Follow the Leader	Emerging	Total Commitment	27
Against the Wall	Total Commitment	Firefighting	28
Pulling Through	Total Commitment	Emerging	29
Breaking Out	Total Commitment	Total Commitment	30

Part 6

How Will You Get There?

	FF	EM	TC
FF			
EM			
TC			

Sink or Swim

Firefighting/Firefighting

It is very frightening to be in a Firefighting group within a Firefighting organization. The company is in serious trouble, and you are caught right in the middle. In fact, yours may be one of the groups that is causing the biggest problems.

Scenario

You run the shipping department for a large furniture store. Unfortunately, customers have been complaining constantly about late and incorrect deliveries. Pieces that should be delivered in eight weeks are taking ten and even twelve weeks to arrive. Scheduled deliveries are missed; and when they are rescheduled, most of the order is either missing from the truck or it is damaged.

One problem is that the orders are being entered incorrectly into the computer. Another problem is that your shipping department is losing the second page of a two-page bill of lading so furniture is being loaded onto the wrong trucks. Finally, employees are making careless mistakes.

You might have time to try to address the problems, except that everyone is in meetings all day blaming each other for the mistakes.

Recommended approach

Start with the fundamentals. Do a basic analysis of the defects that are being reported and determine the problems that are occurring most frequently. See if you can find common root causes and take some simple steps to make incremental improvements to close the gaps in the process that led to the errors.

Try to focus on areas that *do not* require participation from other groups. In all likelihood, you probably will not get their participation anyway, and there certainly are things you can do within your own group that will have a tangible impact on the organization's success.

How to position with the group

To position this effort with the group, start by acknowledging what everyone already knows—the whole operation is in trouble and assigning blame will not solve the problems. Explain that while you cannot persuade everyone else to change, and that while things happening in other groups are affecting your group as well, there are things *within your control* that you can address together which will make things easier for the group.

How to position with management

Any break from the constant finger pointing and blaming associated with a Firefighting organization will be a welcome change. You should explain to management that you understand some of the turmoil is being caused by your group, even though they already know this, and that you are taking definite steps to improve the situation. You will be willing to share what you learn with other groups if they are interested, but there are some things your group can achieve on its own.

Your managers should be impressed by your ability to recognize the problem, identify a solution, and take action proactively.

Summary

There is nothing worse than being in a bad situation—except possibly failing to recognize that you are in one. The old Chinese proverb, "The journey of a thousand miles begins with a single step," is appropriate.

Identify the areas most in need of immediate attention. Take small but steady steps and build the stability of the organization to the point where you can begin to address broader, more challenging areas.

	FF	EM	TC
FF			
EM			
TC			

Catching Up

Firefighting/Emerging

The organization as a whole is in the Emerging mode. Some groups are beginning to see positive change taking place and are starting to see tangible benefits from their efforts. Unfortunately, your group is not one of these and is in the Firefighting mode.

You are experiencing problems that are more related to the internal workings of your group than to interface points with other groups. It is no fun being the *problem child*, and you really have to do something about it now before it is too late.

Scenario

Your company manufactures high-end laptop computers. The products are usually of first quality, but every so often defects occur. These are sometimes discovered during your own internal testing, but, more frequently, they are caught by the customer. Several teams have put into place a formal root-cause analysis program that seems to be getting results. In fact, one team has realized a 60 percent reduction in defects in its area!

Several other groups have adapted this approach and have seen similar results. They are even receiving complimentary letters from customers.

Unfortunately, many of these root-cause teams let you know—with varying levels of subtlety and tact—that they have identified *your group* as the root cause!

Recommended approach

If you remember, the unique distinguishing characteristic of the Emerging group is that intact work groups, rather than scattered teams of people, are ready to move forward. In this case, you have a unique advantage because these leading groups will already have completed much of the legwork for you. In the preceding example, many teams have initiated formal root-cause analysis programs that are working well. Why not try to build upon their success!

You can learn from their efforts, and adapt—or even *adopt* outright—the processes they follow for improvement. Do not be shy about accepting help from other groups. It is not a sign of weakness; rather it is a sign of resourcefulness and maturity!

How to position with the group

The people on your team will easily recognize that they are somewhat behind. When problems arise, they are usually traceable to one of several teams including yours. This is as unpleasant for the members of your team as it is for you.

Discuss with the group the fact that there are some issues that need to be addressed to solve the problems facing the team and to bring the group in line with initiatives being undertaken in other parts of the organization.

Point out that the approaches to improvement you will be employing have already been piloted and proven successful in other parts of the organization. Therefore, much of the time-consuming legwork has been done.

And finally, make sure the members of your team understand that success in this effort should make their lives at work more enjoyable and significantly less stressful.

How to position with management

If you find yourself in this position, there is a good chance that you are exploring options because you have been *invited* to do so by your manager. If the rest of the organization has already made strides towards improvement and your team has not, now is the time for you to get your group on track to make improvement a part of its objectives.

Meet with management and explain that you know there are some problems that need to be addressed. You can describe how you have already met with several other groups to see how they have dealt with similar situations, and you are working with one of these groups to adapt its approach to your own team.

You accomplish three things by doing this. First, you demonstrate that you can act proactively, even in a tough situation. Second, you demonstrate your ability to work effectively with other groups in your organization. Finally, you recognize the other groups for the success they have had and for their willingness to help you. This is only fair—they have earned it.

Summary

Being in this situation is not necessarily a result of poor management. Some groups simply have enough time to address change initiatives because of the nature of the work they do.

Groups that are not in the direct line of fire of customer interaction or product delivery may have less urgency in their workday. Because of this, they may have more breathing room to focus on effective change.

The benefit for you is that you can learn from these groups' efforts and build upon the groundwork they have already laid to help initiate similar improvements in your own group.

24

	FF	EM	TC
FF			
EM			
TC			

Desperate Measures

Firefighting/Total Commitment

Uh oh! The rest of the organization has been progressing satisfactorily towards making significant improvements in process, customer focus, and employee empowerment. However, yours is continually singled out as being at fault in major problem areas. When the time comes to look for a scapegoat—and it surely will—guess who will be chosen? Yours is a Firefighting group in a Total Commitment organization.

Scenario

Almost every time employees try to fill a prescription at their pharmacy, the computer shows that these employees are not covered under their company's medical insurance. Representatives from the plan correct the situation on an individual basis each time an employee calls, but the change is not permanent. Employees have to call month after month. The situation is becoming very embarrassing to all concerned.

Employees are beginning to complain loudly to their company's benefits group which is becoming very frustrated at having to solve the same problems over and over again. This is not only impacting morale, but it is also affecting performance because employees spend literally hours on the phone during work trying to resolve these problems.

Your department continues to be at the center of this crisis!

Recommended approach

One approach is to look for a new job. Another is to get your group on track *very* quickly. Do not be shy. Ask for help from every available source. Ask other groups what they have done in similar situations. Beg for help from the Quality group. Bring in help from outside the organization. Do whatever it takes to get your group back on track.

Find someone who has had a similar problem and act quickly to get the situation at least under control, if not solved. Get a handle on the main sources of the problems. See if there are any *high runners* that demand immediate attention and that might help give you some breathing room. See if there are any known gaping holes in the process that allow problems to occur. Then get to work immediately.

How to position with the group

There is a good chance that things are already so far out of control that members of the group will be entirely nonresponsive when you approach them. They may, in fact, view you as responsible for causing the situation.

Do your best anyway. Explain that the group is in deep trouble, and it does not really matter how they got there. What matters now is how they are going to get out. Explain what you have learned about the situation, how it can be addressed, and what steps you are going to take together.

Once again, be certain the group understands that success in this change initiative means an end to the scathing phone calls they have been receiving hourly.

How to position with management

At this point you are fighting for your professional life. Go to your leadership and explain that you understand the problem, you are going to do whatever it takes to get it resolved, you have discussed it with your team, and you have all made the commitment to make things happen.

Summary

This is really your worst nightmare professionally. If the rest of the organization is in an advanced state of performance and you are not, it is probably for one of two reasons. Either you ignored the warning signs for too long or your management did.

If it is the first case, you had better get to work now. If it is the second case, you may want to skip a few levels on the hierarchy and make your proposal to higher management. In either case, this is the time for risk taking because if you remain even remotely near the status quo, you will likely get fired.

25

	FF	EM	TC
FF			
EM			
TC			

Blazing the Trail

Emerging/Firefighting

This is a very common situation in many organizations. As a whole, the organization is in the Firefighting mode. But even in a Firefighting organization, individual work groups can be at a more advanced level. In this case, your group is in the Emerging phase.

Things are not at their best all of the time, but you do not seem to be as confused and reactive as other groups are. In fact, you seem to have some spare time to work on improving your situation in a formal, focused way.

Scenario

The motor vehicle division in many states is frequently the brunt of jokes by comedians and talk show hosts. And, for the most part, this is true in your state as well.

However, your office is the exception. While many of the commonly perceived problems, like long lines and uncaring, automaton-like staff, are still somewhat present, you have involved the staff in your office in a series of meetings to help identify new approaches to address these issues.

And your efforts are beginning to work. In your manager's most recent staff meeting, your office had the highest performance rating *and* the highest customer satisfaction rating in the state! Your peers are approaching you to ask you exactly how you have been achieving such great results.

Recommended approach

Build upon the success you are having in involving the team towards enhancing performance. There is nothing that makes you more likely to succeed than having already succeeded. The group already knows what is

103

possible, and the recognition you have gotten so far (and, of course, shared with the group) will spark them to do even more.

Select another tangible area to address, involve the group, determine how you will implement the improvements and how you will measure your success. By doing this, you will become recognized as an organization that incorporates positive change into its normal way of business.

How to position with the group

Explain to your group that the rest of the organization is struggling, and it should help out where it can because of the great job it has been doing. Other groups can learn from what the team has accomplished and try to implement similar changes themselves.

The group also has the opportunity to break new ground and take even greater steps forward, because it is recognized as being innovative. Identify the next area to work on and point out to your team how success in this next venture will continue to make their lives at work more enjoyable and will enhance their overall value to the organization.

How to position with management

Point out the interest you have received from other groups to learn about your current improvement approaches. Explain that you already have plans to help support these groups in their attempts to implement change.

Also explain that you have already identified other opportunities for improvement, which will also be applicable in other groups. You have already talked to your own group about piloting this new initiative, and the results should be just as compelling as on the previous project.

You are a hero for blazing the trail initially, you are a hero for volunteering to help other groups, and you are a hero for proactively selecting the next area to address.

Summary

This situation presents you with the potential to have a profound impact—not only on your group—but also on the whole organization. By achieving measurable, repeatable improvement in a specific area, you demonstrate not only the tangible results, but also the fact that improvement and successful change *can* take place in the organization.

You are blazing the trail into new territory here. Enjoy it!

	FF	EM	TC
FF			
EM			
TC			

Forging Ahead

Emerging/Emerging

If you cannot be a Total Commitment group in a Total Commitment organization, this is the next best place to be. While the organization is not at the highest level of performance, it is at least moving forward steadily. Yours is an Emerging group in a Emerging organization.

Because you are in tune with the rest of the organization in terms of improvement and focus on performance, you do not have to *sell* your ideas to anyone. An awareness of the importance of change has already permeated the organization, and you are simply doing your part (preferably more than your part) to help incorporate the changes more effectively.

Scenario

The operations division of a cellular phone provider has consistently been showing superior results. There has been a constant sharing of ideas and approaches among the different groups, and this informal *community of understanding* of best practices has helped the organization as a whole maintain its leadership position in the company.

There is still a fair amount of turmoil, and day-to-day emergencies still occur, but there is a general sense that the division as a whole is beginning to come together.

Recommended approach

Continue to focus on specific, tangible areas you can address, but be sure to continue to attack them one at a time. The focused change approach is still necessary because the amount of *real work* you have to do still prevents you from spending too much time on extra activities.

You should definitely continue to coordinate your plans and efforts with other groups so that you do not inadvertently duplicate effort, or worse, implement conflicting approaches that might have the effect of canceling each other out.

How to position with the group

Explain to the group that much of the work it has been doing has been recognized by the rest of the organization and some has even been adopted as a best practice. As it turns out, other groups have also been investigating new areas, and there are some actions they have identified that can be applied in your group as well.

You can then involve the team to help select from this list and seek its input on how best to implement these new initiatives, while at the same time begin looking ahead to see what can be accomplished to evolve your own performance systems.

How to position with management

Because most—if not all—groups in the organization will be speaking a common language with respect to change and improvement, there is not a lot of selling necessary here. Rather, it is more a matter of positioning what you are planning to do next in the context of a larger picture. In fact, in an Emerging organization, this kind of coordination is one of the primary roles of the management team.

If you are going to adopt something from another group, explain why this is appropriate for your team's focus and how you plan to make it work in your own group. If you are going to take on something new, describe why this is the right piece to attack at this time in your group's evolution and how it will be applicable to other groups after you have worked out the implementation details.

Summary

This is an exciting situation in which to work. While it is not as orderly as a Total Commitment environment, there is enough movement forward to indicate what the group might achieve in the future.

Also, the benefits your work will provide to the rest of the organization will have an impact well beyond the scope of your group's own success.

	FF	EM	TC
FF			
EM			
TC			

Follow the Leader

Emerging/Total Commitment

This situation is somewhat similar in approach to the Emerging/Emerging case. The only difference is that your group lags a little behind the rest of the organization in implementation. While your situation is not nearly as severe as in a Firefighting/Total Commitment configuration, it does require you to play a little catch-up. Yours is an Emerging group in a Total Commitment organization.

Scenario

As a result of a major reorganization, your Customer Service group is now part of the Operations organization. While "re-orgs" can be a little unnerving, you actually find yourself somewhat excited about being part of this function.

The Operations department is highly regarded inside the company, as well as outside the organization from customers who always highly praise the quality of its service.

You expect a smooth transition into the new organization because your group also has a history of focusing on opportunities for improvement and positive change. You are quite pleased with the results of this reorganization, and you feel that your group will integrate well into this department and will be able to make even greater strides than before.

The Operations department has an extremely well thought-out, systematic approach to all of its key functions. This approach is clearly communicated and deployed throughout the organization and is what you had ultimately hoped to convince your prior management team to implement in your old department.

Recommended approach

If the preceding example—where you have been *absorbed* into a Total Commitment organization—is similar to your own case, be thankful that you have the good fortune to be part of an organization that is doing things the way they should be done. Find out where the disconnects or gaps are in your current approach and use the resources that will certainly be present in the new organization to help you achieve success in this area.

If you find yourself in this situation in an existing organization, it is possible that you have been a little lax in following the new approaches it has been deploying. You should take a look at the approach for the firefighting group in a total commitment company in **Chapter 24**; however, you do not have the job-threatening urgency of that situation.

How to position with the group

You have had good success in your own group that has provided a foundation for further opportunities. You have also had additional success in other parts of the organization which will help you in areas that you have not had the time to deal with yet.

Fortunately, the other groups in the organization have piloted initiatives in these areas and have developed a comprehensive system that you can adopt with very little impact to your current work load. This will help you be far more productive and effective in the future.

How to position with management

You have been making incremental improvements to your processes, and you are ready to take the next step. The work being done in the rest of the organization is directly applicable to what you are doing. You are going to work with the representatives from the other groups, identify the interface points, and get your group in line with broader systematic approaches.

Summary

You are fortunate to be in this situation. You can take pride in the success you have had in your own group while benefiting from the broad systematic approach which has been deployed in the rest of the organization.

It should be a fairly easy step to make the transition—groups that have successfully incorporated change into their business operations generally have a high level of flexibility and adaptability.

	FF	EM	TC
FF			
EM			
TC			

Against the Wall

Total Commitment/Firefighting

This is about as frustrating a situation as you can find at work. You try to make changes in your own group, but as soon as you tell others outside the group about them, they all gang up on you for wasting your time when there is important or urgent business to attend to.

The organization is in a Firefighting mode; yet because of the nature of your group, or because of your leadership, your little corner of the world is fine. In fact, it is better than fine, it is great. You are a Total Commitment group in a Firefighting organization.

Scenario

The company is a division of a large multi-billion dollar corporation. It manufactures pumps and systems which are in high demand by a number of markets. Sixty- and even seventy-hour work weeks are not uncommon as people struggle to simply keep afloat.

You know what it would take to help the rest of the organization to progress, but no one has any time to listen. And even if they had the time, they would not have the patience to do anything now. They are all stressed out from too much pressure and too many hours.

Your group, though, has none of these problems. In fact, yours is the only bright spot. People are envious—even resentful—of your success, but you are not satisfied. There is still more room to improve, and your team knows it, too. In fact, you have some definite plans for what to do next.

When you present your ideas to the boss, he says, "Hmm...it sounds like you have a lot of spare time. Why don't you help the other groups get caught up."

Recommended approach

Go ahead with your plans for broad-based change inside your own group, but be discreet. Address anything you do with an eye for how it can help the rest of the organization solve its problems and help whenever you can.

Limit any visibility until you have tangible, measurable results and a clear implementation plan that others can follow if they wish to.

This may sound a little sneaky, but the alternative is to follow the lead of the rest of the organization and do nothing. If you have brought your group to the Total Commitment level, doing nothing will not even be an option for you. You would sooner leave the organization. And you might just do that anyway.

How to position with the group

You have done extremely well to this point, and you have the results to prove it. Unfortunately, everyone else is not at the same level. They do not have the time to listen to you so you can help them. You should continue to move forward and show the organization what is really possible.

Your group probably understands its unique situation as well as you do. Build upon the pride that comes with being the best.

How to position with management

Tell your management team *nothing*, absolutely nothing. What usually happens in this kind of situation is that rather than getting support, you will probably get an invitation to abandon all of your improvement efforts.

By all means, do whatever you can to help the rest of the organization. But any broad-based initiatives within the group should be kept within the group. Then, as the benefits of your effort and your approach become obvious, your phone will begin to ring with requests for help.

Summary

In this situation you have many difficult decisions to make. Is it worth the effort to try to get anything started? Whom should you involve? Is it easier to get forgiveness than to get permission? Should you try to find another group to work in? Or another *company*?

The fact that you are reading this book now means that settling for less than excellence is not an option for you. So plan your strategy very carefully, make sure you collect the necessary data to demonstrate your success, and then go out and very quietly start a small revolution.

29

	FF	EM	TC
FF			
EM			
TC			

Pulling Through

Total Commitment/Emerging

When you work in a Total Commitment group that is part of an Emerging organization, you can have a strong impact. The rest of the organization is beginning to understand how a systematic approach to work, change, and improvement can enhance performance and effectiveness.

Your role is to bring your experience to the table to help the rest of the organization avoid the many problems that may arise on the way.

Scenario

You are the general manager of a hotel which is part of a chain of over a hundred other properties. At the last big general managers meeting, everyone shared the progress being made in the improvement initiatives launched several months before.

One person talked about a new thrust in employee satisfaction that had significantly reduced the turnover rate among employees. Another presented a formal root cause analysis process that had reduced guest complaints by over 50 percent.

In the time since that meeting, you have taken a more holistic, broad-based approach, integrating many of these ideas into a comprehensive system for leadership.

Recommended approach

At this level you are ready to begin using a broad-based approach, like the Malcolm Baldrige National Quality Award criteria—a nationally recognized model for business success—for self-assessment and for implementing an overall systematic approach to running the business.

Because the rest of the organization will be taking somewhat smaller steps in the same direction, your group will be seen as the one integrating all of the independent components into a complete, systematic approach.

How to position with the group

Explain that, as a team, you are going to begin to put together, into a comprehensive system for running the business, all the pieces you have been working on over the last few years.

Along the way, you will be able to help other groups by sharing your expertise and experience. The progress you have made has been recognized throughout the organization, and you are being called upon to begin to help other groups implement similar approaches.

As the scope of their understanding of the business increases, the opportunities for them will also increase.

How to position with management

There are several things you will want to share with your management, and all of them are good!

First, you are already beginning to support other groups that are trying to adapt your existing programs to their own unique needs.

Second, you are embarking on an initiative to merge many of your most successful programs into a complete, systematic approach. You expect major breakthroughs in performance and effectiveness from this new approach.

And finally, you will be prepared to share what you learn with the rest of the organization as your team continues to demonstrate tangible results.

Summary

You are in a position in this situation to lead the organization into a new way of doing business. Most of the other groups are now aware of the benefits that effectively deployed change can bring them, and you will be setting the example for how to integrate the various improvement initiatives into a comprehensive, repeatable system.

	FF	EM	TC
FF			
EM			
TC			

Breaking Out

Total Commitment/Total Commitment

If you are in this situation, you are the rare exception—and you are quite fortunate, too. Your group is at a very high level of readiness and is recognized as a strong contributor to the whole organization. The organization itself is in particularly good shape as well, with outstanding, measurable performance. Yours is a Total Commitment group in a Total Commitment organization.

Of all the nine possibilities, this one is by far the most enjoyable in which to work. The organization is running smoothly, the different groups are working together in unison, and the *warring silos* and *us-and-them* attitudes prevalent in so many organizations are virtually nonexistent.

Scenario

You run a restaurant which is frequented by many regular customers. Every time customers arrive you greet them by name. They are treated wonderfully and served attentively. This is not only special treatment for your regular customers; this is also standard operating procedure.

The food is served promptly and is always hot because whoever is in the kitchen when the order is completed brings it to the table. There is no "Sorry, I'm not your waiter..." syndrome here.

Each team knows what it does and how it helps create an outstanding dining experience, and everyone works together to make this happen.

Recommended approach

In this kind of company, you can start at the top and deploy change and improvement initiatives across the organization.

A top-down deployment, which leads to failure in most cases, will actually work here because of the alignment among all of the component groups. Make sure that the goals and objectives are adequately communicated and understood. You will also need to be there to assist the groups that may still be lagging behind on the readiness curve.

How to position with the group

Very little selling needs to take place. Change—meaning change *for the better*—is a standard part of the work environment. In fact, there is probably time allocated for exactly this kind of activity.

Just explain what is happening, what the specific objectives are, and solicit ideas on how they can be implemented effectively.

How to position with management

Once again, there is not a lot you have to do that is very different from what you have already been doing. Take responsibility for your fair share of the initiative's work load, explain that you will coordinate with the other groups that may be involved, then get to work.

And be grateful that you work in this kind of environment.

Summary

If you are truly in a Total Commitment organization, then you are in an enviable position. However, you potentially face one of the most frustrating impediments to change: success.

Be certain that the organization is actually successful because of a clearly defined, systematic approach to business and not just a dose of serendipity. Many companies confuse results with success. This is only the case when the results are sustainable over time and are the outcome of a sound approach that has been systematically deployed.

Take a minute and determine for yourself which is actually the case in your organization; and, if things are really the way they should be, ensure that they remain that way by incorporating a fact-based continuous improvement model so the organization will continue to benefit from your experience in a positive way.

Part 7

Tying It All Together

31

Deciding What
to Work On

Where do you start?

You have learned about the model of Organizational Maturity™. You have identified your group and company readiness levels. You have studied the recommendations and examples. What do you do next?

There are two basic steps to initiating successful change, whether at work or in your personal life. First, determine what you want, then figure out how to get it. By now, you should have an understanding of the Organizational Maturity™ model to help you implement change under a variety of challenging circumstances. Next, you will determine what to work on first.

Start with what is most important!

When working with our clients to identify opportunities for change, we advise groups that they *should not* focus on areas that will add the most points to their assessment score, or that will get them the highest visibility, or that will help them win a popularity contest within the team. What they *should do* is begin to focus on the areas that will help them enhance performance and effectiveness in their own group and, hopefully, in the broader organization as well.

Possible areas to address

The areas to address for improvement and change can be as varied as the types of organizations themselves. They can be simple and direct, or complex and involved. Of course, the overriding factor should be the *needs* of the organization balanced against the *readiness* of the organization. The method you use to select these areas should be rigorous and comprehensive to avoid overlooking any areas which may be important but not obvious.

In our two-day intensive workshop, *Business Improvement That Works!*, participants use a formal process based on the Malcolm Baldrige Award criteria to assess their organization and identify the areas that will help improve performance and effectiveness. By combining this approach with the Organizational Maturity™ model, the participants are able to develop achievable plans to address these areas in a suitable period of time.

In fact, we commit up to two hours on the second day for the teams to select the actions and develop their preliminary plans. What results is a strong sense of accountability to successfully implement these actions.

Presenting this workshop for several years to a wide variety of corporate, public-sector, and educational organizations has given us the opportunity to see several hundred change and improvement ideas which have been successfully implemented.

The following six examples, organized by broad category, are typical of the types of actions the groups have undertaken. Some of them are basic ideas which may seem somewhat elementary if your organization is at a high level of readiness. Others are more far-reaching with a significant potential impact on the organization.

1. Leadership

- Involve a cross section of employees to help clearly define the group's mission and values and establish a method of communicating them to the rest of the organization.
- Establish a formal bimonthly meeting with all employees to provide information about the company's major accomplishments, challenges, and progress towards long-term objectives.

2. Strategic planning

- Write a five-year strategic plan and formally review and update it every three months.
- Modify the employee appraisal and compensation system to more closely align with the long- and short-term objectives from the strategic plan.

3. Customer and market knowledge

- Develop a comprehensive system for assessing customer satisfaction to help understand and predict future purchase behavior.
- Establish a new marketing function to involve selected key customers to participate in the product design phase.

4. Information and analysis

- Identify five key business measures to assess the health of the organization and establish processes to acquire and communicate this information to help improve decision making.
- Select three noncompeting companies that share similar manufacturing technology and establish a benchmark consortium to identify each of the company's best practices and share this information among the participating companies.

5. Human resource focus

- Establish a formal employee development program which identifies key employees in the organization and provides a succession of positions and assignments for them that will help maximize their long-term contribution to the organization.
- Set up one functional group in a self-directed team format to serve as a pilot program for determining the feasibility of using this approach throughout the organization.

6. Process management

- Identify key business areas and develop formal processes to provide a consistent approach to accomplishing the organization's goals.
- Implement a formal system to perform root cause analysis on defects and incorporate the resulting preventive actions into the work process.

Exercise—Selecting Areas to Address

By asking yourself the five questions that follow, you can determine the parameters which will form the foundation of your change initiative.

Study the questions and discussions that follow. Write your answers on **Work Sheet 10** on **page 121** to begin the thought process. As you consider the answers, try to focus on a single area you can address to improve performance and effectiveness in your group. On the bottom of the work sheet, write this idea in the form of a complete, detailed statement. This will form the basis of your Action Statement.

1. What are the long-term objectives of the group?

Refer back to your mission statement and strategic plan. Use the knowledge of the group's purpose and objectives to help you identify the areas that need to change.

2. What are the group's most serious roadblocks?

What types of roadblocks have made it difficult for the group to achieve its objectives? These may be internal or external to the group, but remember that it is difficult to change what you cannot influence directly.

3. What issues have my customers raised?

Often your customers will identify the issues you need to address, and often they will do this in no uncertain terms. Be careful not to confuse the symptoms (what the customer sees) with the problem (what you can fix).

4. What needs to take place now?

Finally, trust your gut feelings. In all likelihood, you already know what needs to change; you have just had a difficult time understanding how to make it happen. As a leader in the organization, your instincts are as valuable an indicator as any other input.

5. What is the scope of the action: the entire group or a part of it?

Remember, you can only affect the part of the organization over which you have some direct influence. If you manage a group of ten employees, your scope is clear—it is the group.

If, on the other hand, you are a vice president with responsibility for a group of 1,200 people, you may want to pilot the initiative in one part of the group before implementing a full deployment.

The size of your group and the readiness levels of its components will help you make an appropriate selection.

Work Sheet 10—Where Do You Start?

Instructions: Answer the following questions to help you target some issues you may want to address in your group. Then select an area and write the Action Statement to form the foundation of your change initiative.

1. What are the long-term objectives of the group? _____

_____

_____

2. What are the group's most serious roadblocks?

_____

_____

3. What issues have my customers raised? _____

_____

_____

4. What needs to take place now? _____

_____

_____

5. What is the scope of the action: the entire group or a part of it?

_____

_____

Action Statement _____

_____

_____

Exercise—Validating the Action

Now that you have identified an area to address, you must validate the action on several levels. To start, consider the following questions to ensure that you have selected the best area. Study the questions and explanations that follow. Write your answers on **Work Sheet 11** on **page 124**.

After completing the work sheet, you may need to make some adjustments to your action statement. Or perhaps throw it out and start over again. Remember, once you understand your group's level of readiness, selecting a suitable and achievable action is the most important part of deploying your change strategy.

1. How does the action correspond to my level of readiness?

Even after reading about the serious pitfalls that await groups who mismatch approach and readiness, many people, in their sincere desire to bring about change, will select an area or scope that is much too ambitious considering the readiness of the group.

2. Why does the action make sense?

Sometimes your own *inner voice* can do as good a job of validating your selection as can a formal pros and cons or force field analysis. Think about what you have selected. Does it make sense considering the level of your group? Does it make sense based on your current work load? Is it the *right* thing to do?

3. What would my boss think of the action?

Despite our discussion about empowering yourself, the fact remains that life is generally easier when your manager lends support to your action and when he feels compelled to do so based on the obvious merits of the action. Other people, whose support you need, will be able to determine how important the initiative is to your boss by what he says or does and by what he *does not* say or do.

4. What would my "other" boss think of the action?

Because companies are frequently organized around key processes or key customer accounts, many employees find themselves in a matrix management situation with two or even three managers. When you select your action, make sure you consider the level of support you will receive from all of your managers.

5. *What would the members of my team think of the action?*

Many times, the issues that you think are important are very different from what the members of your team would suggest. Without their input, you may be allocating time and resources into an area that is not as critical as others. Without their support, the task will be difficult, or perhaps impossible. Involving the team in both the selection and implementation of your action will greatly improve your chances for success.

6. *How will the results be measured?*

This is *extremely* important. If you are going to undertake an initiative that will require people to change their behavior, use valuable resources, and divert focus from the *real work* of the organization, it is reasonable for people to expect that their efforts will produce results and that the results will be tangible and measurable.

As you determine how to measure the effectiveness of the change, make sure that you isolate the specific variable that corresponds to the change. Too often, when someone claims an X percent improvement in one area, or a Y percent reduction in another area, the response is, "How do you know it was *your* idea that caused this— it could have been a dozen other things!"

Having compelling, objective data is the only real proof that your efforts and approach are valid. It will enhance your credibility and help make it easier for other groups to benefit from your work.

7. *How is the action transferable to other groups?*

If the area you are addressing has benefits which are limited to your own group, it may be more difficult to gain support from management. If, on the other hand, the work can serve as a pilot program that other groups can adopt later on, it becomes much more viable.

Part of the benefit of working in a large organization is the opportunity to learn from other groups' best practices. Make sure you do your part to contribute to the knowledge base.

8. *How can the action be made a permanent part of the work process?*

Any improvements you make are only as good as your ability to incorporate them into the normal patterns of work. If the new methods require too much special treatment or attention, then they will not be followed.

Make sure that it is relatively easy to adapt your current work processes to the new model.

Work Sheet 11—Validating the Action

Instructions: Answer the questions and update the action statement.

1. How does the action correspond to my level of readiness?

   _____

2. Why does the action make sense?_____

   _____

3. What would my boss think of the action?_____

   _____

4. What would my "other" boss think of the action?_____

   _____

5. What would the members of my team think of the action?

   _____

6. How will the results be measured? _____

   _____

7. How is the action transferable to other groups?_____

   _____

8. How can the action be made a permanent part of the work process?

   _____

Updated Action Statement _____

   _____

32

The Five Steps to Well-formed Actions

Overview

At this point many well-meaning change initiatives self-destruct. Here is why.

When I left my corporate life behind to begin work with a larger and broader group of organizations, I had the opportunity to clean out my office and review years of accumulated memos, organization charts, and training manuals.

As I flipped through the pages of these manuals from a variety of programs in management, marketing, negotiating, and other business areas, one common theme was evident. In the syllabus of each of these programs, there was a comment somewhat like this:

> At the end of this program, you'll develop a comprehensive plan of action that will get you so excited and motivated that you'll call home to announce that you'll be late because you're at work implementing this exciting new plan *immediately!*

I then turned to the back pages of these manuals, where I had carefully and painstakingly followed the instructors' directions and developed my plans. As I reviewed these plans two, five, and ten years later, I realized I had not implemented a single one of them.

The method of action planning in each of these programs involved the following three steps:

1. Think about what you learned today.
2. Choose something to work on.
3. Now, make a detailed, comprehensive plan.

In retrospect, it is no surprise that I did not act on any of these actions. I was asked to spend considerable time deriving a detailed plan for something I had spent about one minute selecting.

In the rare case where I actually took some time to select a really good area to address, I often tried to tackle something that was much too ambitious. Inevitably I gave in to the overwhelming odds against success and abandoned the effort.

How, then, can we identify a good area to address, refine it so that it is achievable, and develop a realistic implementation plan? The first step is to understand what a well-formed action is.

Organizational change is like personal change

Several years ago, I had the opportunity to participate in an extended program in the field of Neurolinguistic Programming, an approach to understanding human behavior, identifying patterns of communication, and facilitating personal change.

One of the overriding themes in this program was that in order to accomplish any meaningful change in behavior, it is critical to clearly identify what the desired change is, determine if it is achievable, and ensure that it is something you really want.

As I learned more and more about how to apply this approach, it became clear that these exact steps were essential in affecting organizational change as well.

Why plans fail—even with the best intentions

Once people—or organizations—decide on what to do to improve, they almost immediately define a plan of how they are going to accomplish this change. Frequently, it is a very detailed plan, with individual objectives and specific milestones. Unfortunately, most people jump into the planning stage much too soon without really defining what it is that they are trying to accomplish.

What good is having a detailed plan if you are not doing the *right* thing? This is an example of the parable that practice does not make perfect—*perfect* practice makes perfect.

Exercise—Well-formed Actions

A key to successful change is to make sure that the intended outcome of your action is well-defined. Read through the discussion that follows for the five steps to well-formed actions. Then on **Work Sheet 12** on **page 130** apply these statements to your updated Action Statement from **Work Sheet 11** on **page 124** to ensure that your action meets the five criteria for determining well-formed actions. If necessary, update the Action Statement to reflect any changes.

1. State the outcome in positives

When attempting a change initiative, the outcome should always be stated in positives. In other words, describe what you are *going* to do—not what you are going to *stop* doing. It is far easier to *do* something than to stop doing something. Any time you stop a behavior or an activity, another one must supplant it.

For example, you might want to stop taking five days to respond to customer complaints. Great, but what will you do instead? Perhaps you will respond to customer issues within twenty-four hours. Now the objective is restated in a way that is positive and achievable. You now have a target to shoot for.

2. Explain how the action is within your sphere of influence

Too many groups undertake programs that are far beyond their capabilities and resources. When they inevitably run into the roadblocks of what they lack—resources, knowledge, and influence—the program crumbles under the weight of its own good intentions.

Carefully examine the area you are going to address. Can you accomplish your objectives with the resources in the group? Do you have access to the necessary resources which may lie outside of your direct span of control? If not, do you have adequate personal power—an influence base into other groups—so that you can get what you need, when you need it?

Answering these questions before you start will help ensure you succeed in making change happen.

3. Specify a context in which to implement your action

This is the step in the process that invites you to take your noble goal of solving world hunger and constrain it to the point where you can make an impact. For example, you may be able to leave a can of food in the mailbox on the day the letter carriers hold their annual food drive.

Your grand idea may be to perform a root-cause analysis on all product defects. But if you actually do this, you probably would not have time to develop more products. Balance your desire to improve the way you do your work with the practical requirements of running the organization.

Specifying a context in which to deploy your improvement initiative will give you the opportunity to pilot a new approach in a controlled environment. When you achieve initial success, you can broaden your implementation as appropriate.

4. Clearly define your outcome in terms of desired behaviors

This may be the most important of the five areas, but it is also one of the most difficult. That is because it requires you to have a very clear picture of what you are trying to accomplish. You must define the outcome in a specific, measurable way so that there can be an objective end point.

It is also important to specify your outcomes not only in terms of results and targets, but, more importantly, in terms of desired *behaviors.*

How will the group members act differently when the initiative is successfully deployed? How will they think differently? How will they feel differently? Only when these facets of the initiative are defined, can you get a total picture of what you are setting out to accomplish.

If you have a clear idea of the outcome, you will always have a target to aim for. If you do not have this understanding, you may go off in the opposite direction and think you are on the right track when you really are not.

You may also make some progress, get halfway there, and think you have achieved your objective when you have not. Or, you may meet your goals and keep right on going because you do not even realize that you have arrived yet.

With a clear picture of where you are going, you may *zig* and you may *zag*, but you will ultimately get where you are going. At worst, you may reevaluate your initial goal and realize that it may not have been exactly what you needed.

Ultimately, you will be like an airline pilot who may be *exactly* on course to the final destination only 5 to 10 percent of the time, but who always gets you there.

5. State how the outcome would benefit the organization

The final test is to ask yourself if this is really what you want. It is like the old adage, "Be careful what you ask for...because you might get it!"

Make sure that the effort you are undertaking is really worth the commitment of time, money, and resources. Sometimes the cost of the cure is significantly greater than the impact of the problem. Be certain that you are not spending $100,000 to solve a $50 problem.

Also consider the impact the new approach may have on your team and on other groups with whom you interact. Make sure that everyone will be able to function effectively under the new system.

A fast-tracking young executive was once invited to attend a retreat for people who were expected to be among his company's top 100 executives in twenty years. One of the first exercises they were asked to do was to describe what their life would be like in twenty years when they were the top executives of the company.

They drew a picture of what they expected their house to look like in twenty years. They wrote essays describing what their relationships with loved ones would be like. They filled out a week's worth of planning sheets to describe what a typical workweek might be like.

The interesting thing about this story is that after completing these exercises, about 25 percent of the people in attendance packed their bags and went home. They had drawn in their minds an accurate picture of what the future would look like, and they had the foresight and good sense to realize that it was not what they wanted.

Be certain that you examine your intentions carefully and deliberately to ensure that you get the outcome that you desire.

Work Sheet 12—Well-formed Actions

Instructions: Review your objectives for change on **Work Sheet 11**, **page 124**, and apply each of the five tests to the updated action statement. Explain how you have considered each one. Then reformulate your new action statement if necessary.

1. State the outcome in positives _____

_____

_____

2. Explain how the action is within your sphere of influence

_____

_____

3. Specify a context in which to implement your action

_____

_____

4. Clearly define your action in terms of desired behaviors

_____

_____

5. State how the outcome would benefit the organization

_____

_____

Updated Action Statement _____

_____

_____

33

Ensuring Success and Next Steps

What steps do you need to take next?

You have determined your work group's level of readiness, examined it in context with the readiness level of the organization as a whole, selected a high-impact area to address, and refined the scope and definition of your action to ensure success.

There are a few other areas you should analyze to help you achieve the results you desire.

Measure

Measure. Measure. Measure. As has already been mentioned, it is important to select measurable areas to address. Without facts and data to back up your assertions that real improvement has taken place, all you are is another person with an opinion.

With clear, objective proof of your success, not only will you and your team receive the credit you deserve, but also other groups will recognize the value of your approach and will be willing to adopt what you have accomplished into their own organizations.

Avoid committees

What frequently happens when improvement ideas are presented to a management committee for its review is that they are escalated up several levels of management for consideration. This can make it extremely difficult to get these ideas implemented in a timely fashion.

If a committee has responsibility for initiating an action, your ideas may never come to fruition. Whenever a group of individuals is responsible for an action—*no one* is responsible for that action.

In addition, sending the action up the hierarchies has its own problems. For starters, if the problem requires significant approval from above, you have probably violated the second of the *Five Steps to Well-formed Actions*—making sure actions are within your sphere of influence.

Keep in mind the old saying, "If you don't want something done, send it to a committee."

Advertise success

Sometimes you can be your own best-kept secret. If you have accomplished something truly commendable in your group, there is no reason to hide it.

If you do not share your success, you will not receive recognition for your efforts, and other groups will not have the opportunity to learn from what you have done. This is not bragging; this is sharing valuable information that others can use to benefit the organization.

Celebrate results

This is an area that is often overlooked. In our effort to manage all of our responsibilities in an atmosphere of *do more with less*, we frequently forget to take time out to celebrate victories. If the team has really accomplished something new or innovative or noteworthy, it is your responsibility to recognize the members adequately.

If the area you selected to address was a good one, the financial benefits you realized should exceed *by far* the cost of a well-deserved celebration. The members of the team will appreciate that you recognize their efforts, and they will be ready to quickly tackle the next area.

Also, along the way, regular recognition of the team as a whole and of the individuals on the team will show them that you understand and appreciate their efforts. Even something as simple as saying, "Thank you. I know you're working hard on this program, and it's beginning to pay off," can go a long, long way to keep the team motivated.

Start now!

Procrastination is one of the biggest inhibiting factors in initiating change. Many times we know what to do, we know why we must do it, but it never seems to happen. We think about all the other things piling up on our desks. We focus our attention on all the crises. We ruminate over past decisions that may not have turned out quite the way we had expected.

We often fail to take action on the initiatives that we have identified to help us find our way out of these very situations. The key is to take action *now*! People seem to have trouble making the decision to start. But in the final analysis, remember that *not* making a decision is, in fact, *making a decision to do nothing at all.*

Empower yourself!

Remember that no one is more committed to seeing your ideas come to fruition than you are. Letting the success for your initiative rest in someone else's hands can lead to serious frustration. While it is always a good idea to keep your manager informed, there are times when it is easier to obtain forgiveness than permission.

Do not waste valuable time by waiting for the situation to be just right. An old Chinese saying exemplifies this: "A man sitting on his front porch can wait a *very* long time for a roast duck to fly into his mouth."

You have gone through a very deliberate process to identify your group's level of readiness, to determine how it relates to the readiness level of the overall organization, to select the type of action, and to zero in on a specific area to address. You have invested too much time and effort to let it drop at this point. So get moving, now!

34

Evaluating Your Efforts

Change is a process, not an event

It is necessary to continually review your progress and evolve your processes. Once you begin to see results from the initial actions you have implemented, it is time to reevaluate your situation to assess the effectiveness of your initial work and determine how best to proceed with any additional changes. This should be done on an regular, ongoing basis—monthly, quarterly, or a time frame that works for you—to ensure that you are at the right level of readiness for the actions you are implementing.

Exercise—Assessing Progress

After you have seen some initial progress from the action you selected in **Chapter 32**, you should evaluate the results of your efforts to see if you are getting the results you had anticipated.

The following ten questions will help you analyze how well you did with your initiative and will trigger important issues you should address when implementing future change. They are a reminder that it is critical to match the readiness level with your approach to change. Use **Work Sheet 13** on **page 138** to make periodic notes on the progress of your initiatives.

1. What was your level of Organizational Maturity™?

It is always important to establish a baseline measurement to understand what the situation was at the beginning of any initiative.

2. What was your objective?

After you completed the five steps to well-formed actions, what was your clearly defined objective? How was it going to impact the group?

. How were you going to measure success?

A major part of establishing any change initiative is to have an objective method for measuring its effectiveness. What were your parameters for determining the level of success?

4. What results did you achieve?

List the outcomes you realized from this initiative, both positive and negative. What changed in the way the group thinks, acts, and feels about the work? Were there any unexpected benefits that came from your efforts? Were there any side effects that you had not anticipated?

5. What factors helped ensure your results?

To help you replicate your success, it is important to isolate the factors that encouraged, allowed, or mandated the initiative's success. What factors in the environment helped? Which individuals offered support, encouragement, or direct assistance?

6. What factors inhibited success?

Since we learn more from our failures than from our successes, it is equally important to understand what impeded the initiative. Again, consider the business environment, as well as any individuals who may have negatively impacted your efforts.

7. What areas did you discover that needed attention?

Typically, attempting change is like peeling away the layers of an onion. As you begin to make progress in one area, you uncover related areas that should be assessed also. These often form the genesis of future opportunities for change.

8. Have you identified any groups that could benefit from your work?

One of the real benefits of the Organizational Maturity™ approach is that it allows teams that may be at a higher state of readiness to lead the way for more broad-based improvement. What groups have you identified that may be ready to adopt your models and approaches—or even better, what groups have contacted *you* to learn more about your initiative because of the results you have demonstrated?

9. Has the organization's level of Organizational Maturity™ changed.

Before determining what, if anything, should be addressed next, it is again imperative to understand the readiness levels of the group and the company to ensure that an appropriate approach to change will be selected.

10. What should your next initiative be?

What now? You want to be careful not to create your own flavor-of-the-month mentality by immediately spawning a new and different program. But there are usually logical extensions that you can implement to enhance your initial work.

In addition, the impact your efforts have had may have brought the organization to a level that can support and benefit from a more broad-based approach. Select carefully.

ork Sheet 13—Assessing Progress

Instructions: Answer the questions regarding progress on your initiative.

1. What was your level of Organizational Maturity™?_____

_____

2. What was your objective?_____

_____

3. How were you going to measure success? _____

_____

4. What results did you achieve?_____

_____

5. What factors helped ensure your results?_____

_____

6. What factors inhibited success?_____

_____

7. What areas did you discover that needed attention?_____

_____

8. Have you identified any groups that could benefit from your work?

_____

9. Has the organization's level of Organizational Maturity™ changed?

_____

10. What should your next initiative be?_____

_____

35

Final Thoughts

The Organizational Maturity™ model was derived from actual experience with what works and what does not work in initiating change in organizations, not from theoretical, academic research.

If you have come this far, you should have a very clear plan for success in your organization. It is important to remember that organizations are dynamic, living systems. They change over time based on what happens to them, within them, and around them.

The levels of readiness of both the organization and of the individual groups that comprise it will rise and fall over time. Certainly, your own efforts to improve the organization will help.

Come back and revisit the model regularly. Continually monitor the readiness level of the group and the organization as a whole and the impact your efforts are having. Share your success with other groups and consciously work to learn from your failures.

You will have an enormous impact on your organization's success, you will feel more empowered, and you will feel much better about coming to work each day.

Index

How QualityTalk®
Can Help You

Free online newsletter: "Eight Rings: Ideas for Change"

The online newsletter, "Eight Rings: Ideas for Change," presents real-life situations that explain the principles of change and provide specific ideas you can put to use immediately to help bring about meaningful change in your own organization.

To receive a free subscription to this newsletter, call or email your request to us at newsletter@qualitytalk.com. Include your name, company, title and email address. Or fax the order form on **page 147**.

Workshops, training programs, and keynote presentations

QualityTalk programs are energizing, entertaining, and packed full of content. Ron engages his audience through the use of illustrative stories and anecdotes, input from participants, and group exercises. Plus, he even adds a bit of magic to his programs. Through the use of several magic effects, he captures the full attention of his audience and drives home key points that they will remember long after the program is over. Here is a partial list of his workshops, training programs, and keynote presentations:

The Eight Rights of Organizational Influence!™

To remain competitive while continuing to grow and evolve, companies must look beyond the basics of good management and customer satisfaction. Leaders must begin to think like leaders and ask themselves the kind of questions to help them identify and capitalize upon new opportunities. The Eight Rings of Organizational Influence™ provides the keys to help organizations more successfully understand their environment, motivate and retain the best people, and achieve tangible and lasting results!

Business Improvement That Works™

This program presents the concepts of leadership, strategic planning, and customer service in a way that makes sense from the tangible perspective of running a business. You will assess your organization's level of performance, needs for improvement, and readiness for change, and then develop a comprehensive strategy for success.

Breaking Out of the Change Trap™

Successful change programs require a foundation of process management supported by a committed senior management team. If you lack any of these, do not abandon your efforts. In this enlightening program, you will learn how to recognize whether your organization is ready for a broad-based approach; and if it is not, how you can take action towards tangible business results.

Stop Defects!™ The Defect Prevention Workshop

To be truly successful, it is not enough to solve your customer problems with corrective actions—you must get to the root causes and stamp them out with preventive actions. You will learn a series of techniques to help you identify the root causes of product and service defects and identify preventive actions you can implement in your own organization.

Volume book discounts

To receive additional copies of *Breaking Out of the Change Trap*, call, mail, fax, or email your request. The order form on the following page is provided for your convenience. Special high-quantity discounts are also available upon request for use as premiums in sales promotions or corporate training programs.

For more information

In addition to the programs above, Ron also offers other workshops and keynote presentations on customer service and leadership development. All programs are tailored to address the particular needs of each customer.

For more information on any of these programs, call toll free at 800-260-0662. Outside the US and Canada, call 919-847-0662. Email your requests to info@qualitytalk.com. Or mail or fax your request using a copy of the order form on **page 147**. The fax number is 919-847-9041. Check out our web site for additional information at: http://www.qualitytalk.com

Order Form

To: Ron Rosenberg, QualityTalk   Fax: 919-847-9041

Re: Fill out the information below for your request and fax with your credit card information or mail with your check to QualityTalk, Inc.

Date: _____

Name: _____ Title: _____

Company: _____ Phone: _____

Email Address: _____ Fax: _____

Mailing Address: _____

City: _____ State: _____ Zip: _____

❑ Yes, I'd like to receive your free online newsletter, "Eight Rings: Ideas for Change." My email address is listed above.

I'd also like to receive information on the following programs:

❑ The Eight Rights of Organizational Influence!™
❑ Business Improvement That Works™
❑ Breaking Out of the Change Trap™
❑ Stop Defects!™ The Defect Prevention Workshop
❑ Customer satisfaction programs
❑ Leadership development programs
❑ Other _____ (please indicate)

❑ Please send me additional copies of *Breaking Out of the Change Trap* (1-5 qty. @ $14.95 ea.; 6-25 qty. @ $13.50 ea.; 26 or more @ $11.95 ea.)

No. of books: _____ @ _____ = _____

NC residents, add 6% sales tax: _____

Add shipping and handling: _____
(Shipping/handling for 1 book is $4.50; add $.50 for each additional book)
Total Payment (due at the time of order): _____

❑ My check or money order is included payable to QualityTalk, Inc., P.O. Box 99451, Raleigh, NC 27624-9451

❑ Please charge $_____ to my Visa card

No. _____ Exp. Date _____

Signature _____

(Your credit card number, expiration date, and signature is required to ship your charge order.)

"Change doesn't happen by magic...it takes
vision, focus, and a commitment
to personal excellence."
Ron Rosenberg

About the Author

Many companies are attempting fundamental changes in the way they run their businesses, but they are not seeing positive results from their efforts. Ron Rosenberg, president of QualityTalk®, works with organizations to help them successfully implement change to improve performance and effectiveness. A professional speaker, trainer, and consultant, he has presented programs both nationally and internationally.

Ron's background in industry includes engineering management, international marketing, and strategic quality planning, most recently with Nortel as the company's senior manager for quality and training at its Research and Development facility in Research Triangle Park, NC. There, he received the company's highest honor—the Chairman's Award of Excellence—for his leading-edge approach to quality.

Ron served for three years as an examiner for the North Carolina Quality Leadership Award. He presents regularly at major national and international conferences and has published many articles on business improvement, change management, leadership development, and customer satisfaction. He holds an undergraduate degree in computer science from Rochester Institute of Technology and an MBA from New Hampshire College.